The Proper Care of
MARINE FISHES

Scott B. Meyer

Useful Conversions and Equivalents

WATER WEIGHT
1. A gallon of water weighs:

Imperial		USA	
10 lb	4.5 kg	8.3 lb	3.8 kg

2. A liter of water weighs 1 kg or 2.2 lb.
3. A pint of water weighs:

Imperial		USA	
1.25 lb	0.57 kg	1.04 lb	0.47 kg

4. 1 cubic foot of salt water = 64 lb
   1 cubic foot of fresh water = 62.43 lb

GALLON EQUIVALENTS
1 Imp. gallon = 1.2 US gallons = 4.55 liters
1 US gallon = 0.833 Imp. gallons = 3.78 liters
1 Liter = 0.264 US gallons = 0.22 Imp gallons
1 Imp. gallon = 277 in^3 = 4,542 cm^3
1 US gallon = 231 in^3 = 3,685 cm^3

LITER EQUIVALENTS
$$1 \text{ Liter} = 1,000 \text{ cm}^3 = 61 \text{ in}^3$$
$$= 1 \text{ Kilogram}$$
$$= 1.76 \text{ Imp pints} = 2.11 \text{ US Pints}$$

WEIGHT
1 Kilogram = 1,000 grams = 2.2 lb = 35.2 oz
1 Pound = 0.45 kg = 454 grams
1 Ounce = 28.35 grams
1 Hundredweight = 112 lb = 50.8 kg

CAPACITIES
Length x Width x Depth = Cubic Capacity (Volume)
(See under Gallon Equivalents for volumes of these)

MEASUREMENTS
Length x Width = Surface area
1 inch = 2.54 centimeters
1 cm = 0.39 in
12 inch = 30.48 cm = 0.3048 meters
1 m = 39.37 in = 3.28 ft
1 Tablespoon = 3 teaspoons = 1/2 fluid oz
1 Teaspoon = 1/6 fluid oz = 1.3 fluid drams
1 Pint = 16 fl oz = 128 fl drams
1 Fl. dram = 3.7 mils or cc

TEMPERATURE
° Celsius x 1.8 + 32°= Fahrenheit
° Fahrenheit - 32 x 0.556 = °Celsius
Each 1° Celsius change in temperature = 1.8° Fahrenheit
E.g. If the temperature of water is raised 3° C, this will add 5.4° to the Fahrenheit temperature.

ELECTRICITY
Power (Watts) = Current (Amps) x Voltage
Amps = Watts divided by Volts

Contents

Introduction

The desire of humans to keep fishes within the confines of their homes has persisted for well over a thousand years. It probably originated during the early Chinese dynasties, when the first goldfish color mutations must have attracted much attention. In those days the fish were kept in ornate vases and earthenware pots, as well as in outdoor ponds. As the centuries rolled by, fishkeepers became proficient breeders, able to keep many freshwater species alive. The desire

Pseudochromis paccagnellae

native fishes in aquariums. The problems were that too little was understood about the chemistry of water, and there was a paucity of equipment available. With their much larger aquariums, zoological institutions were more successful than the few hobbyists of the time, but even so success was always limited. The London Zoological Gardens opened the first exhibits of freshwater fishes and

to keep marine fishes was also considerable, but all early efforts to do so failed, other than keeping a few species alive for only a matter of days.

Even as recently as the 19th century, zoological societies were struggling to maintain

The two photos on this page show miniature reef aquariums. Beginners are advised to start off with fish-only aquariums before progressing to mini-reef tanks.

attempted to maintain marine fishes as well. Salt water was transported by wagons from the coast, and an elaborate system of blinds controlled the amount of daylight that entered the exhibition rooms. Huge bellows were used to try to intro–duce air into the aquar–iums, but still the fishes died. Ultimately, the society gave up and closed the fish exhibits for a number of years–until more knowledge was gained.

A mini-reef aquarium.

By the early years of the 20th century hobbyists were beginning to truly understand the needs of freshwater fishes, and the popularity of keeping coldwater species– goldfish in particular–started to boom. The knowledge gained from these attempts resulted in the steady increase in the number of tropical species that could be kept. The increase soon become a flood, and a whole commer– cial industry developed around fishkeeping.

A few specialists continued to dabble with marine fishes, but the high costs of obtaining them, coupled with their short life expectancy, invariably saw enthusiasts becoming increasingly dejected. However, institutions were steadily gaining knowledge about the needs of the fishes, and this knowledge eventually filtered through to the commercial side of the pet industry. Better tanks, improved equipment, and more nutritious foods, as well as the all-important development of artificial salt mixes, were beginning to make the keeping of marine fishes a better proposition.

Fish and invertebrates in a mini-reef aquarium. You need some experience before you start a mini-reef aquarium.

During the last decade even greater breakthroughs have been made, to the degree that some species are even being bred in captivity, an almost unheard of situation only a few years ago.

Today you can enjoy the breathtaking beauty of having gorgeously colored fishes in your living room. You can have a mini coral reef and its fishes in all their splendor, rather than having to rely on seeing them only in the movies, on television programs, or in a public aquarium. There is a further advantage to you if you have never kept fishes before. Your mind will not be prejudiced with preconceived ideas gained by experiences based on freshwater fishes. You will be less tempted to overstock your aquarium, and you will be more likely to study the needs of the fishes to a greater degree than might have been the case had you kept tropical freshwater fishes previously. Marine fishes are not as forgiving as marine fishes is not more costly than owning a tank full of freshwater tropicals, but the rewards amply repay this extra cost. There is still much to be learned

Stegastes leucostictus from Puerto Rico.

freshwater fishes if their environment is not as it should be–they die quicker! As the fishes are more expensive, the marine fishkeeper tends to take a healthier regard for the needs of his or her fishes. This makes for a better hobbyist.

It would be foolish to suggest that keeping about keeping marines in captivity and they remain a challenge. This gives an owner a tremendous sense of achievement once an aquarium is up and running smoothly. There is considerable scope for the observant newcomer to add to the existing bank of information on these

Hippocampus kuda, the Yellow Seahorse.

fishes, the more so if specialization is practiced. Another advantage of the marine aquarium is that many other life forms can be accommodated in saltwater tanks than is the case with freshwater species. Indeed, you could devote an entire aquarium to invertebrates and it would still be a fascinating and colorful unit. They certainly deserve a book of their own.

In this book it is hoped that you will find all of the basic information you will need to understand in order to establish a viable ecosystem for marine fishes. You should, however, also locate a reliable pet or aquatic store that keeps a number of marine tanks on display. With judicious use of books and the dealer's advice, your entry into this branch of fishkeeping should be rewarding,

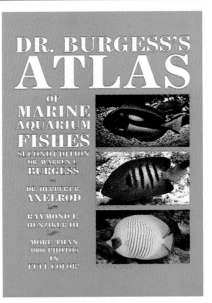

Dr. Burgess's Atlas of Marine Aquarium Fishes

TFH style # H-1100

The biggest and most colorful identification guide to saltwater aquarium fishes.

with a minimum of difficulties along the way.

It must be stressed, however, that marines cannot be taken for granted as can goldfish, for example. You must look after them to a much higher degree and be prepared to devote some time to studying their needs. By so doing you will not be disappointed.

Environment

If there is one thing that any aquarist must know about, it is water. This is especially so if you wish to keep marine fishes. The subject is discussed in more detail in a later chapter, so here we will review it in a more general manner.

You have no doubt seen rivers or canals in which dead fishes are floating on the surface. Along with these will be all manner of garbage such as cans, plastic

Many hobbyists keep invertebrates of various types with their fishes, but some invertebrates may cause problems. The beginner might be better off with a separate invertebrate aquarium.

materials, bits of wood, and the dead bodies of other animals. The water has a dirty greenish brown look to it, and there are the telltale rainbow rings that indicate oil and other chemicals have been discharged into it. There may also be the frothy white scum of industrial waste floating on the surface as well.

I doubt that the idea of drinking from this would appeal to you. This being so, just imagine trying to live in it. Now, rivers are relatively small bodies of water when compared with the seas and oceans of the world–which comprise a little over 70% of our earth's surface. Yet even in these vast expanses of water we see fish dying from pollutants dumped into them by tankers, factories, and sewage works. If parts of seas containing many billions of gallons of water can become lethal to the fishes, then it stands to reason that any tank of water you could possibly have in your home is a potential death trap unless you take regular measures to ensure that it is not.

THE NATURAL WATER CYCLE

Whether in an ocean or in a mountain stream, water undergoes a natural system of cleansing that enables it to support many forms of life. It commences its cycle when the heat of the sun evaporates the water from the surface of the oceans and lifts the water, minus its salts, into the air as clouds. These pass over land and become cooled, forming rain that falls onto the land. This water, together with that created by seasonal melting of high altitude snows, thus begins its long journey back to the seas and oceans. As it passes over differing types of rock formations it dissolves these, some

This mini-reef is in the home of Prof. Dr. Cliff Emmens, the outstanding marine writer.

more than others. When it flows over areas of organic matter it becomes soft and acidic, while if it flows over chalk it becomes alkaline and hard. These aspects are most important to those who keep freshwater fishes. As leaves fall into the water, and as fishes and other organisms die, they decay and fall to the bottom of the river, ultimately creating mulm. However, before this happens, many of them are either eaten by other large organisms or decomposed by microscopic life forms. A chain, from the infinitesimally small to the very large, is created– the one being dependent on the other.

The water is oxygenated at its interface with the air and, via this same surface, potentially toxic gases in the water are released. To aid in this process, the water passes over rocks and waterfalls which agitate it. Any local build-up of organisms pathogenic (disease causing) to the fishes is overcome, in the main, by the fact that the fishes are constantly moving downstream. If

A magnificent mini-reef aquarium with fishes and anemones.

the fish population increases beyond the level of natural balance, then disease within the population, or an increase in the fish's predators, keeps their numbers within tolerable levels. As the fish population falls back, so the predators die in larger numbers, and this repeating cycle forms the natural system of survival.

The many plants that grow in rivers and lakes are important in the cleansing process because they absorb, as food, dangerous chemical compounds. These they convert into their own structure, which in turn is itself a food for many fishes. The rivers eventually flow back into the sea, where their properties are considerably changed. The oceans and seas contain large quantities of sodium chloride (salt), and this increases the density of the water. Other minerals are also present in ratios differing from those found in fresh water. These, collectively, alter the amount of oxygen that the water can dissolve. The vast depth of an ocean results in other changes. For one thing, the temperatures tend to remain more static. The pH value (see the chapter on water properties) also remains more stable. Light intensity levels are further examples of the more stable environment created in the seas and oceans.

These differences in the two types of water, salt and fresh, have meant that fishes and other organisms have had to evolve quite different ways of living in them. In theory, you might think that if marine waters are more stable in their properties, this should make keeping marine fishes easier than those of fresh water, where the properties are variable and thus need to be related to the fishes living in them. However, the reverse is the case. Because small volumes of water, such as even the largest of aquariums, can change their properties so quickly, this means that such changes could have a deleterious effect on the fishes. Freshwater species are more able to cope with the fluctuations in

With so much sea water around us it might seem a good idea to use this in aquariums, but things are not that simple. We do not all live near the sea, and

An anemonefish in its anemone—an interesting sight, but not always easy to achieve.

aquarium water because in their natural environment such changes are often found seasonally, if not over a twenty-four-hour cycle.

Marine species thus require great stability in the properties of the water in which they live.

even if we did there would be problems. Coastal areas are the worst waters in terms of pollution. Furthermore, sea water rapidly loses its properties when transported in small containers. The complex balance of life within sea water only retains equilibrium when the water is in vast volumes. This being so, the marine aquarist must try to artificially create an acceptable environment for the fishes. This is possible by using specially prepared commercial mixes to make synthetic sea water.

SIMULATING THE NATURAL CYCLE

It is clearly the object of the aquarist to try and simulate the natural water cycle within the confines of an aquarium unit. This will mean the following:

1. Ensuring that there is sufficient oxygen in the water to support the number of fishes it contains, making due allowance for the fact that they will grow and have differing body sizes.

2. Ensuring that potentially toxic substances, such as ammonia and its compounds, are removed, or at the very least held down to a livable level.

3. Ensuring that nitrogenous wastes created by the fish's fecal matter, by uneaten food, and by dead organisms is removed so it cannot build up to result in polluted water. What cannot be removed must be converted into harmless chemicals by some means.

4. Ensuring that potentially pathogenic bacteria are removed or held at tolerable levels.

5. Ensuring that the fishes are not overcrowded.

6. Ensuring that the fishes receive a diet that they will accept, and in sufficient quantity to meet their nutritional needs.

Meeting these various requirements in terms of the water properties can be achieved in one of two ways. Either a percentage of the water must be removed and replaced at very regular intervals or the water must be treated in some way that will achieve the objective. To keep replacing quantities of water is not only a time consuming chore, but it is fraught with prob–lems.

Will the temper-atures of that added be equated to that remov-ed? Will this remove sufficient of the harmful properties the water in the tank has gained? Will the fishes be stressed by the constant disturbance to their home?

ecosystem. You must use mechanical means that will enable you to circulate the water, then fit filters into the circulation system to remove the impurities. Periodically, you can remove small quan-tities of the water in order to dilute any harmful proper-ties that may not have been removed

The outstanding feature of this tank is the anemone and the anemonefish (upper right in photo). With a enough experience you can successfully maintain a tank like this one.

The answers are such that removing quantities on a very regular basis is not a satisfactory means of trying to establish a workable

by the cleansing system. This should create an environment that, at least, meets the minimum needs of the fishes.

EXPECTED LOSSES

It is within the nature of animal hobbyists that they will quickly reveal any success they achieve but are far less inclined to document their losses. Let us consider this aspect so you know what would be reasonable for you to expect. As a novice you will clearly make mistakes; on this account alone some, hopefully not all, of your initial fishes will die. When an aquarium is first established it often suffers from what is termed "new tank syndrome." The extent of losses from this aspect will reflect, to a large degree, the efforts and patience you have shown in preparing the water.

This said, even the best-prepared aquarium will suffer losses. Many marine fishes are wild-caught specimens. Some of them will be old fishes that were not long for this world anyway–the rigors of being caught and transported will prove too much for them to cope with. Conversely, very young fishes may not be strong enough to cope with the traumas that are an inescapable part of capture. Some fishes will already be suffering from a problem when they are caught, while others may become so shocked that they never fully recover. Some will be unable to withstand the numerous water changes they might experience. Finally, the treatment they receive from the eventual dealer who sells them to you will play an important part in whether or not they survive. You are not alone in terms of the sort of percentage of losses you might incur. If a bird breeder decides to take on rare species about which little is known, high losses are commonplace. Marine fishes still represent one of the more difficult areas of fish-keeping, so losses will be considerably higher than if you were to keep goldfish or koi, two of the most robust species of fish.

The major difference is that goldfish are relatively inexpensive when compared to marine species, so each loss of marine fishes therefore tend to fall into two camps, those that learn quickly and endure, those that don't and give up very quickly.

You can have an aquarium without marine fishes, just marine invertebrates, but this is much more complex and is not recommended for the beginner.

hits you (more specifically your bank balance!) much harder than with most freshwater species. Marine enthusiasts

Marine fishes in home aquaria often live much shorter lives than they do in large commercial or public aquariums. The following will give you some idea of the differences in expected longevity. An angelfish may survive fifteen years in a public aquarium, whereas in your tank it will do well to attain five years of age. Puffers and snappers are good for twelve or more years in public displays, but yours will probably expire in half this time. In general, your local zoo will keep their fishes alive anywhere from 25-300% longer than you are likely to. This will reflect their greater knowledge, their much larger aquariums, and, possibly, the fact that they deal with suppliers of long standing who are more diligent in how they capture and transport the fishes.

Most hobbyists do not, in truth, keep a tally of what their hobby is costing them. When all is said and done, it comes down to just how much you love the magnificent beauty of marine fishes and the challenge of providing for them. You must relate the life span of the fishes in your tank to their cost and the available funds you can devote to the purchase of equipment. You can certainly minimize your losses by adopting these few simple rules.

1. Do not purchase any fish until you have experimented a little with water properties, then set up a tank that is allowed to become "mature."

2. Have more than one aquarium set up so that if any fishes become ill you can isolate them for treatment.

3. Commence with the largest aquarium you can afford. The bigger it is the less rapidly will changes occur in the chemical properties and temperature of the water.

4. Invest in the best quality salt mixtures, and be sure you follow faithfully the manufacturers' instructions for their preparation.

5. Invest in high quality filter systems and other mechanical or biological aids.

6. Establish a good relationship with a all fishes before adding them to your existing display.

7. Do not attempt to mix many species together, or to risk

Algae such as the *Caulerpa* species shown here are the most common plants in marine aquariums.

reputable dealer, then stick with that store. Do not shop for the cheapest fishes; they will invariably be the most expensive in the long run. Quarantine overstocking your aquarium. Start with the less costly species and keep only a few of these while you gain practical experience. Add fishes only one, two at most, at a time.

Always remember that your aquarium is a complete ecosystem. In the wild environment things do not change wild bring about calamities–and they will do likewise in your aquarium. Observe your fishes so that you know how they feed and what

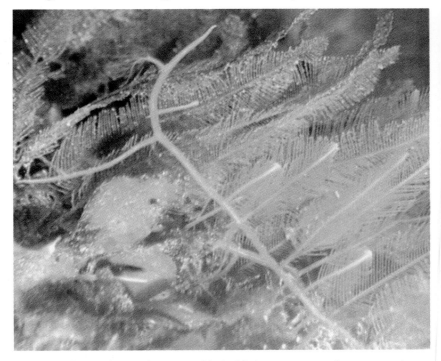

If your marine tank gets the proper kind of light, you can easily grow marine plants like this one.

suddenly, nor do fresh species suddenly appear. Things happen on a very gradual basis. In this way the fishes have the best chance to adapt to the changes being made. Sudden changes in the their normal day to day behaviors are like. If these start to change, it usually indicates a problem of some sort. Keep a record of your losses and note the tank conditions when they happened. Only by

The larger the marine tank you buy, the easier it will be to take care of.

recording and comparing your percentage of losses over a period of time are you truthfully able to judge your progress and success rate.

Hopefully, this general over-view of the saltwater environment will have prepared your mind for the more specific data that is contained in the following chapters. However, never assume that there is only one way to achieve an objective. Always be prepared to listen to the advice of other hobbyists–if what they say seems to be based on common sense. There is still so much that is unknown about marine fishes, especially about their breeding habits, that clearly it will be the beginners of today who will eventually unravel many of the problems that will enable hobbyists of the future to attain higher rates of success.

Tank Selection

The selection of a tank suitable for housing marine fishes should be considered more carefully than one to be set up for freshwater fishes. Water rusts some metals, and salt water does this much more quickly. A marine tank must be made from materials that do not rust, so items like angle-iron frames should be avoided. Even stainless steel will be attacked over a period of time, so its use is not recommended for your marine fish's home. The

most commonly available choice will be an all-glass aquarium, which may feature some decorative strips fitted to the outside to resemble a frame, but they are not really necessary because the all-glass unit can look very smart by itself.

An alternative material is plastic, the highest grades of which are better than glass in some very important regards. Less expensive plastics will tend to scratch easily and become yellow with age, so you should convince yourself to purchase the best quality tank from the outset. You should also seriously consider purchasing one or two spare tanks. These can be of lesser cost and maybe smaller. They will be useful as quarantine or isolation tanks, even if your initial thoughts are not geared toward obtaining more fishes.

SIZE AND SHAPE

The size of a marine aquarium, and to a lesser degree its shape, is most important. Buy the largest one you can afford–there is no upper limit. The larger the tank the more readily it will retain its water temperature in

For starters get the largest tank you can afford and start with the fewest fish.

the event of a power failure. Likewise, it will not easily overheat during very hot weather, which the small unit might do even if it is not being heated. It will also be far less susceptible to water chemistry changes than will the smaller tank. Given these aspects, the minimum size you should be thinking in terms of will be a 29-gallon unit—and this would be a very small tank for marines. Its dimensions would be on the order of 90x38x30cm (36x15x12in).

Apart from the purely practical considerations of water chemistry and the size of the tank, you should also bear in mind that the size will be important in other ways. All fishes require a certain amount of territory in which they feel safe. Some species that will happily co-exist in a large tank may become extremely

Most aquariums, whether all-glass or acrylic, are rectangular in shape, although other shapes also are available.

antisocial if placed in a smaller unit. Timid fishes must have the space and hiding places in which to evade the more aggressive species. All species are seen best when they have sufficient room in which they can freely move. A goldfish in a bowl will hover almost motionless for long periods–a real boring exhibit. Put that same fish in a large aquarium and it will swim around exploring and browsing. It will feel better and it will look more interesting from your viewpoint. The same is true of your marine fishes.

With regard to the shape of the tank, the best advice is to obtain a regular oblong (rectangle), at least until you know whether or not you wish to become a more involved enthusiast. This shape provides a good viewing area and is easily situated, and it is easy to work out its capacity in the event you need to treat it with medicines. It is also the least expensive option because most tanks are this shape. You can also purchase L-shaped corner units that look very attractive. More unusual shapes will be those with bowed fronts, triangular models, and round tanks. These do not always display the fishes too well, as they may distort their shape or size, depending on which angle you are viewing them from. They are also more expensive.

You can purchase complete system units that hold the ancillary equipment, so you can see that there is no limit to the amount of cash you can spend. You could, of course, make your own tank, but such units are rarely as sound as those that are made commercially. I would recommend that, unless you are especially able, you purchase one of the latter ones.

It doesn't take much to start a marine aquarium. If you can afford it, you can buy a complete system together with all the ancillary equipment, all attractively presented as a piece of modern furniture. It is a living picture.

If you select a large tank be sure it is substantially built. It should contain the additional feature of at least one cross brace of glass, and maybe corner braces as well. These will provide added strength where it is needed most. Water exerts a considerable pressure, and such braces will prevent front-to-back bowing. The corner braces also will provide support for a glass cover, a most useful feature for the tank. This will prevent fishes from jumping out of the tank, and at the same time reduce the amount of water lost through evaporation and the amount of dust that might otherwise settle on the water's surface.

TANK LOCATION

You should ponder the location of your tank carefully; numerous factors must be taken into account.

1. It should not be near a window where it will be subject to strong sunlight. Apart from possible excessive algal growth, the main drawback is that it will adversely affect the water temperature. It may make it too hot in the day, and then there will be a rather sudden drop overnight. Such fluctuations will do your fishes no good at all. For the same reason you should avoid placing the tank over or near a central heating radiator or forced air duct (air conditioning). It is much better if the tank is in a dimly lit area of a room, because in this way you have total control over the amount of light it receives via the lighting system you choose.

2. Avoid placing it near or opposite a door. This may subject it to cold drafts in the winter or to excess noise should the door suddenly slam. Most fishes are very sensitive to noises: loud bangs could shock the more timid members of the fish community.

3. A vital consideration, especially with any tank in excess of 124cm (4ft), is the strength of the floor. More than one large tank has suddenly crashed through the floor under the weight of the completed setup! With a very large tank you should find out

Aqua Modules are complete units made for the specific purpose of decoration. This marine aquarium was designed to be viewed from three sides.

where the floor joists are and then place the tank so that its weight is spread out as much as possible. If there is the slightest doubt, it would be prudent to seek the advice of a competent builder or engineer.

4. If at all possible, put the tank as near an electrical outlet as you can. This will save you from having to trail wires around the room. These look unsightly and, depending on their length, can cause a small loss of power. It would be better to have an electrician wire in a new socket or two close to the aquarium and have them protected by

This built-in marine unit also serves as a night light.

a ground fault interrupter.

5. As you will no doubt wish the pleasure of spending quite some time viewing your fishes, it follows that the aquarium is best situated near an easy chair so that you can sit back and let your mind wander off to those warm tropical reefs.

You may decide that you wish to have the aquarium as a room divider. This will look really attractive, but it is not without its problems. Be sure to consider the avail–ability of electricity to run the equipment and the need to have food and other items close at hand. It is also more difficult to arrange a display such that it is attractive from all viewing positions around the tank. Such dividers are best when they are very large and mounted on brick bases with tailor-made overhead canopies– after the fashion of see-through fireplaces.

STOCKING LEVELS

Stocking levels can be viewed in two ways. You can either decide approximately how many fishes of a given size you wish to keep, and then purchase a tank of suitable size,

This marine aquarium was made to be viewed from all directions.

or, more probably, you will need to work out how many fishes the tank you can afford will hold safety.

I am sure you will appreciate that two tanks of identical measurements can vary significantly in many ways once they are set up. One may have a higher temperature than another (thus less oxygen content), or one may have been prepared with a better salt mix, or one may have more intense light on it than another. The water chemistry of each will reflect these aspects, as well as the forms of decoration that have been used, how well the owner has pre-cleaned everything, and how well the filter and other equipment perform. Also, some fishes are more active than others and will pollute the water more quickly. In short, you cannot lay down hard and fast rules as to how many fishes a given tank will support, because there are too many variables.

This fact must be stated so that you do not assume that the recommendations shortly to be given are absolute; they are approximate guides based on the experiences of many hobbyists and experts. You should always work on the generous side so as to ensure that there is no possible risk of overcrowding the tank. If, as you add more fishes, the conditions in the tank start to deteriorate, or if the fishes become more aggressive with their co-inhabitants, this fact, rather than theoretical stocking levels, must be your guide to reducing their numbers or purchase of a bigger tank or better equipment.

The best advice you could use would be that if your calculations suggest a stocking level of four fishes of a given

A marine aquarium can be built into your wall.

size, then start off with two, or at most three. This way, if things go wrong your losses will at least be minimized. If nothing goes wrong you will be extremely pleased you heeded this advice! There are two ways in which you can work out stocking levels. One is based on the surface area of an undergravel filter, if this is used; the other relates the size of the fish to a particular number of gallons of water.

1. Filter Area. Allow 1cm of fish (not including the tail) per 120CM² of filter area (1 in per 48 in²). If you have kept freshwater fishes before, note that the area is that of the filter, not of the water surface. In practice, these are often the same, as it is recommended that undergravel filters, to be fully effective, should cover as much of the bottom as possible.

The top of an inactive fireplace can also be a good location for a marine tank.

2. Water Volume. Allow 2.5cm (1 in) of fish per 5 US gal. (4 Imp. gal., 19 liters). In order to be a bit more accurate, you should reduce the theoretical tank capacity by about 10% so as to allow for the volume of the rocks and/or other decorations and adjust

for the fact that you will not fill the tank to the brim.

This stocking level will allow for the growth of However, if you decide to keep a few large fishes, do not be tempted to increase this stocking level, as bigger

Aquariums can be built into existing furniture.

your fishes over the first few months. If all goes well, and with gained experience, it will be possible for you to increase this stocking level as time goes by. fishes tend to be less "efficient" than smaller ones–they use up a higher percentage of oxygen and expel a greater amount of nitrogenous wastes.

Pieces of coral called "living rock" can form the basis for mini-reef aquariums. As the rock comes to life with plants and marine invertebrates, it decorates itself.

Electricity and Lighting

ELECTRICITY AND LIGHTING

As I am sure you are well aware, electricity and water are a deadly combination. This being so, you must pay particular attention to safety aspects when dealing with your marine aquarium.

This is probably even more applicable with this type of setup because salt water corrodes wires and connections much faster than does regular fresh water. The rule of

The marine tank in the home of the famous Belgian explorer Guy van den Bossche.

Aquariums are dependent on electrical devices to keep them functioning smoothly. Since electrical equipment and salt water make a potentially lethal combination, aquarists have to pay attention to basic safety procedures when setting up and performing routine maintenance in and around the aquarium.

never placing your hand into the water when the power is on should never be forgotten–even a safe system can go wrong, and your body could just be the quickest route for the electricity to go to earth! All fittings should be of the water resistant type made specifically for aquarium use; they should be checked and cleaned on a regular basis for salt that may have crept onto them (usually from evaporated spray).

Safety Measures

It is worthwhile mentioning a few very basic safety measures that should be taken when electrical appliances are being used in connection with any aquarium units. Probably the biggest single element to insure your own safety and the long life of the electrical equipment is this: pay attention to the manufacturer's directions that come with the equipment. Some of the things that manufacturers say in their instruction sheets are common-sense recommendations dealing with the use of electricity around water, and those things should be paid attention to exactly because they're common-sense recommendations. Other strictures given by manufacturers in their instruction sheets refer specifically to the particular pieces of apparatus that they're packed with, and they too should be taken into account when setting up the equipment.

A very important element where any heat-producing pieces of equipment such as lights and, especially, heaters are concerned is the consideration of making sure that the outlet into which they and the other pieces of equipment are plugged doesn't get overloaded. Heaters normally have a higher wattage rating than other pieces of aquarium equipment, and the total power they draw can start to add up to a point beyond what should be comfortably used with a standard home wall outlet. Therefore it pays to keep track of the total wattage being drawn at any given outlet and to split the load up among more than one outlet if possible. Certainly you'll want to resist the impulse to stick in "just one more plug."

It can't be said too often: when you're dealing with electricity and water, be careful.

It will be useful to purchase a wire tidy from your aquarium dealer. This should be insulated to guard against potential electrical leaks. It definitely is worthwhile to obtain a ground fault interrupting multi-outlet powertap that can be plugged into your wall outlet if your wall outlet is not already GFI-protected.

Another view of the marine aquarium in the home of the Belgian explorer Guy van den Bossche.

THE ROLE OF LIGHT

Although a great deal is now understood about the importance of light in the aquarium, it is true that there is probably more that still remains to be discovered. If we consider a few general aspects first, these will be useful in helping you to decide what sort of light you will need in your marine aquarium.

The most obvious statement with regard to fishes, invertebrates, and plants is that they require light in order to be seen. Organisms that live in the unlit depths of the oceans display little, if any, color. Color itself is the result of two factors, the presence of pigments in the skin and the reflection of light from pigment-free cells in certain animals. In the latter case, parts of the natural light spectrum are absorbed (long waves) while short waves (violets and blues) may be reflected back to the viewer. For these reasons, some fishes will appear one color in a certain light, but another when the light intensity or angle changes–the latter may also affect the actual distribution of the pigment granules, so that the fish or invertebrate can literally change color before your very eyes.

Living organisms also tend to react to light in either a positive or a negative manner. Roots are photonegative, but stems and flowers are photopositive, i.e., they grow toward the light source. In the seas the light source is, of course, the sun, so kelp, anemones, and similar attached living forms will grow toward the surface. This can present the aquarist with problems if the aquarium receives natural sunlight. The plants will grow toward this light source, and as it will often be coming from the front of the tank, the plants will grow toward the front rather than upward, as the hobbyist would wish.

However, even fishes are photopositive with respect to their body position in the water, e.g., their back is held toward the light source. If they receive excessive light from the front panel of the tank, they may start to swim at a slight angle, an undesirable situation for the viewer.

Plants, such as algae, need a good light source in order for them to survive. Light is required for photosynthesis to

This huge sea anemone and other marine invertebrates are kept alive by the actinic lighting. This photograph was taken by actinic lighting alone.

take place.
Photosynthesis is the
process whereby light
energy plus carbon
dioxide, plus hydrogen
(from the water) are
converted to organic
compounds that make
up the cell structure. The
plants are browsed upon
by certain fishes as well
as other organisms,
which in turn are eaten
by predators, which die
and fertilize the plants,
thus completing the food
cycle. Plants also release
oxygen during the
daytime and, although
they reverse the process
at night, there is a
positive oxygen surplus
over a twenty-four hour
period.

To a large degree light
controls the feeding
habits of many sea
creatures. Some are
nocturnal (active at
night), others are diurnal
(active during the day),
while yet others are
crepuscular (active
during dawn or dusk).
The breeding habits of
many animals are

Without the utilization of special lamps and lighting, most mini-reef aquariums could not survive. This photo was made with actinic light, the same lighting which keeps the fishes and invertebrates in such excellent condition.

directly linked to the amount of daylight they receive. Fishes are included among these animals, especially in the non-tropical zones of the world.

The actual chemistry of the water is determined in no small degree by the duration and intensity of light. Light affects the life cycles of millions of microorganisms–their death creates pollution and their life creates food. Under dark conditions, anaerobic (non-oxygen breathing) bacteria multiply. The result is an increase in the toxic properties of the water, both by soluble particles and by gases. Finally, light, in the form of the sun and its location with respect to the equator, determines the temperature of any natural body of water. This will then control the oxygen content of the water.

If you consider all of these factors and their permutations with each other, it immediately becomes apparent why there remains so much that is still beyond our knowledge.

YOUR LIGHTING NEEDS

You will find that, as in many areas of animal husbandry, your lighting needs will represent a compromise, unless you decide to become a committed specialist. In the latter instance your only thoughts are to provide as near to ideal living conditions as possible for those fishes you wish to keep. However, for most hobbyists the need is to create a pleasing aquascene in which the fishes can be readily seen and are therefore illuminated with this in mind. This is where the compromise will become necessary.

If you prefer a very well lit aquarium you will find it will also become very rich in algae, which you may not wish to have. If you want the best view of your fishes, the lighting is best placed toward the front of the tank–but this, then, is where the algae will live. The best place for the algae is on the sides and back panels of the aquarium, but this will mean that the lights must be placed farther back, which does not provide for the best viewing of the fishes' colors. If you prefer a more dimly lit aquarium, yet wish to feature algae for the fishes to feed on, you are desirous of two opposing situations. The dimly lit aquarium will also be an ideal place for blue-green and brown algae to live; these are both undesirable, at least from a general maintenance viewpoint.

Some fishes are from very well lit areas of the world, such as shallow coral reefs; others prefer somewhat deeper waters where the sunlight is less intense. Fishes from temperate climates will not need as much light as those from tropical areas. More accurately, they will require seasonal variations in the intensity and duration of the light.

Even those species not noted for shyness, such as this *Chromis viridis,* should be provided with areas in which they can seek refuge from the light occasionally.

You must therefore review the type of aquarium display you want and the types of fishes to be stocked. It is always better that you restrict your choice to fishes of a given area

This *Holocentrus adscensionis* from the Virgin Islands has a special night color pattern.

of the world and a particular habitat. In the former case you can then concentrate your efforts toward a deeper understanding of the needs of the fishes of that area (say the Pacific or the Indian Oceans or the Caribbean Sea). Better still, try to have fishes from the same type of environment–coral, midwater, and so on.

It is only by such methods that we will really begin to appreciate the more delicate requirements of marine fishes, and thus may be able to supply the conditions and stimuli most needed for breeding.

Once you have made a study of the likely lighting needs of your fishes, you can then work out what would be the best permutations to achieve the desired visual effect, yet enable the ecosystem you have created to function as near as possible to normalcy.

YOUR LIGHTING OPTIONS

The options open to the aquarist, assuming natural daylight is not to be a major consideration, will be between three types of lighting:

1. Tungsten (Incandescent) Lamps.

The major advantages of these lights are that they are inexpensive to install and cost very little to replace. Their disadv–antages, however, greatly outweigh any benefits they may give. Their oper-ational costs are high when compared to fluorescent lighting, and the life of a bulb is relatively short. They generate rather a lot of heat–which is unwanted by you, thus is wasted electricity.

This *Holocentrus rufus* from Bonaire has daytime coloration from artifical daylight-colored lamps.

Because they are hot, these bulbs carry the distinct risk of imploding in the event that water should splash onto them. While the light they give out is not that bad, it can be greatly improved upon with the specialized lighting now available in fluorescent form, and which can be geared to very specific needs. Tungsten bulb fittings are no longer common-place within the hoods of commer-cially made units. The latter are slimmer and more attractive. Finally, unless special tungsten bulbs are purchased, they are not designed for horizontal use, but for vertical suspension.

2. Fluorescent Lighting. Most of the drawbacks with tungsten bulbs are overcome with fluorescent, or strip, lighting. These are very economical to run, will last longer than you should actually use them, and generate very

little heat. They are thus much safer, apart from the fact that they are not wasting current on the production of unwanted heat. You can select from These are beneficial for growing plants as well as showing the fish colors to best effect. However, they are rather less bright than regular tube lights.

many types of bulbs to suit your particular needs. For example, some tubes emit light in the very short and the very long wavelength ends of the natural white light spectrum. These are the violet, indigo, and blue short waves and the longwaved red-orange. In terms of their actual ability to illuminate (efficiency), they are more costly to operate than would be, for example, cool white tubes. To overcome their lack of lighting power, you can run other fluorescent lights in tandem with them, so as to provide the sort of lighting that

The three tanks shown on this and the facing page are identical except for lighting. On the facing page only Gro-Lux lighting is used. The tank above uses actinic lights and fiber optics; the tank below features Gro-Lux and fiber optics.

appeals to you and yet is beneficial to the inhabitants of the aquarium.

Blue lights, which are especially strong toward the ultraviolet end of the light spectrum, will be of advantage to numerous those species that prefer a slightly less intense light, you can create them quite easily. Arrange your decorations so as to form caves, ledges, and other recesses that would be found in the coral reef or

This is Hamilton's light enhancer. The electro-white reflector is available from aquarium shops.

invertebrates. But do follow the manufacturer's recommendation as to their use, otherwise they may be potentially harmful to other organisms living in the aquarium which are beneficial.

Fluorescent tubes give an even spread of light, thus avoiding the creation of unwanted shadows. However, if these are needed for rocky outcrops of any ocean. The major drawback with this form of lighting is that the starting mechanism (the ballast or choke) is rather heavy and the tubes will need to be replaced each year, at least. This is because they lose a certain amount of their fluorescence with usage. Even so, they are still among the most popular lights used these days by all aquarists.

3. Spotlights. There are numerous types of spotlights available for use over aquariums. Unlike fluorescent lights, which are suspended only inches from the water surface, spotlights must be placed at least 31cm (12in) above the water. This means that conventional hoods cannot be used-but special lamp holders and overhead hoods are produced to house these lights.

They are all rather powerful (they range from 80-200 or more

This Energy Saver drop light can be raised or lowered to change the density and coverage of light.

watts) and thus have a high operating cost. They are best used where you need a light that must penetrate well down into a deep tank and thus are generally only used by those aquarists with very large aquariums. High pressure sodium lamps are similar to those used for street lighting and so yield a slightly orange light. Quartz halogen, otherwise known as metal-halide, bulbs produce an extremely intense, bright light that must be used with care. Mercury vapor lamps also produce an intense light well suited to the deep aquarium and are less expensive than the previous type.

Apart from the penetration aspect of spotlights, they are also extremely useful for creating visual effects. You can train the light, with the aid of decorative reflectors, to given areas of the tank. This is not easily done with fluorescent lights. They do, of course, generate quite a lot of heat–a definite drawback. Furthermore, they should be balanced carefully so as to provide the correct spectrum of light. If you wish to use spotlights it is suggested that you discuss this at length with your dealer first and see which ones are recommended (if any at all) based on the size of the aquarium you plan to install. He may be able to show you the effect of various lamps by holding them over one of his display tanks, or there may even be some in use.

DURATION OF LIGHT

It has already been mentioned that this must be based upon the species being kept and their known requirements. Bear in mind that even though some species may come from tropical areas, this does not mean that they automatically need a great deal of light. They may be fishes that spend much of their time in the shadows. As a very general rule of thumb you should think in terms of having the lights on for about 12-15 hours per day for tropical species, and 10-12 hours for temperate region fishes, but increasing this to 12-14 hours during the summer.

AVOIDANCE OF "LIGHT PLUNGING"

I use this term to describe the situation created when light is either turned on or off suddenly. This will cause the fishes to panic momentarily. In this

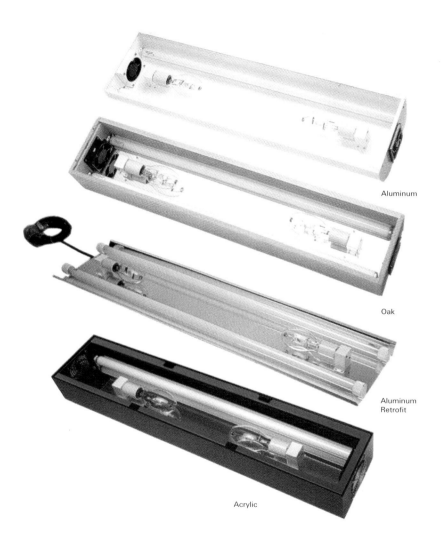

Aluminum

Oak

Aluminum
Retrofit

Acrylic

Energy Savers makes a full line of lights and reflectors to satisfy most aquarist needs. Here are four of them.

state they may dash themselves against rocks or the glass, and in so doing injure themselves. It will most certainly also stress them–the last thing you want to happen. You can avoid the situation in one or two ways. Either switch the aquarium lights off some minutes before the room lights are turned out, or fit a dimmer unit to certain lights so that they go off gradually The latter is easily the better option. You may also leave a low wattage blue tube, or a tungsten bulb, on overnight.

We know just how important sunlight is to fishes, but there is a scarcity of data on the effects of moonlight. Moonlight surely must play a part in the life of some fishes, which is why a small blue light may be beneficial.

Seahorses use their prehensile tails as holdfast organs.

AMOUNT OF LIGHT

From what has already been discussed, you will appreciate that it is indeed extremely difficult to say just how much light a given aquarium should receive. What is true is that many aquariums receive a greater intensity of light than would be the case under natural conditions, this being a result of the enthusiast's desire to have everything well illuminated.

If bright illumination is used, try to balance this

by providing a number of dark, shady areas. See how the fishes react to the two regions. By trial and error you should be able to strike a balance between that preferred by the fishes and that acceptable to your viewing pleasure. If you wish to be sure that there will be healthy algal growth in your aquarium, you should commence with about 3 watts of fluorescent lighting per US gallon. This can be adjusted up or down according to results. It is assumed that the tank is of rectangular shape. A 29 gallon tank would thus require about 90 watts of lighting. Tube lighting is usually available based on 10 watts per 30cm of tube length. A 29-gallon tank would normally be 93cm (36in) long, thus you would need three 30-watt tubes (rounded off to the nearest workable wattage). However, these may not fit under the hood, in which case you would require a different arrangement.

Trumpetfish, *Aulostomus maculatus.*

It must be stated that differing authorities vary dramatically in the wattage per gallon they recommend. In a recent survey the author found these recommendations ranged from 1.45 to 5.9 watts per gallon, a rather wide sweep. What is suggested here represents a balanced view that should ensure

Striking a balance between enough and too much algal growth is a process of trial and error. As seen here, the growth of algae can become rampant.

good algal growth without becoming rampant. It allows you to use three types of fluorescent tubes so as to provide a good color spectrum range, yet enjoy a well illuminated tank that will show off the colors of your fishes to best advantage. Bear in mind that if you use a warm white type of light and later replace it with a standard light, the colors of the fishes will appear to have changed.

If you should decide to purchase a nontraditionally shaped aquarium (which is not recommended for the novice), you will immediately create problems in calculating the lighting needs of the unit. In this text it is assumed the unit will be rectangular, so the relationship between the surface area and the water volume will stay reasonably constant. If you purchase a tall tank with a limited surface area, all calculations for equipment become more complex. You will need intense spot lights to illuminate the lower levels of the aquarium, and this will mean a higher surface temperature. You will need a more powerful aeration system to overcome the poor surface-to-air interface. All in all, it is best to stick with regular shapes until you have gained considerable experience. This will be preferred by the fishes, as it will give them the optimum of useful swimming area.

If you plan on keeping corals, once you've graduated past the beginner stage, you will need special high-intensity-lighting. The bodies of corals have symbiotic algae that are responsible for producing much of a coral's oxygen and also many of the minerals necessary for building reefs. Beginners should not keep corals unless they get detailed instructions and help from an advanced hobbyist.

Garden Eels, *Heteroconger halis.*

Heating

Unless you are planning to keep coldwater marine species, you will require some form of heating in your aquarium. As with lighting, there are a number of aspects to consider when deciding on the heater needed for your particular aquarium. Heaters come in a range of wattages and in a number of types. They must also work in conjunction with thermostats that regulate how often they come on or switch off. The vast majority of aquarists will use "in tank" heating by means of wire coils encased in glass. This text is written with these

Thermostatically controlled fully submersible aquarium heaters are available from most pet shops. Photo by SRL.

people in mind. However, for completeness we should perhaps review the full range of options so that you are at least aware of them.

1. *Space Heating.* This method is possibly less expensive to operate when a large number of aquariums are situated in the same room. It has the advantage that no heating appliances are placed in the aquarium. There are no wires necessary for the heating of the tanks, so space heating arrangements have obvious benefits. However, to attain the required temperatures for tropical marine species, the room would have to be very hot–which would make working in it most uncomfortable.

The initial cost of the heating apparatus, be this forced air, heated water, oil radiators, or whatever, would be costly. Additionally, this method does assume that the temperature required in all the tanks is to be the same, which may not always be the case. It is thus unlikely that such a system is of practical use to the average hobbyist even if he does have a number of aquariums.

2. *Heater Pads.* This form of heating has the advantage that tanks can be heated individually, thus at different temperatures. Pads are useful if a sterile aquarium is required. However, much heat is lost via the glass base of the aquarium and to the air around the tank. Such a system can hardly be considered cost effective.

3. *Undergravel Heaters.* These have the advantage that they do not suffer from heat loss to the air or to the tank base, but they may heat the substrate

Tank heater pads normally are not used for heating aquariums.

HEATER WATTAGE

It might seem academic how powerful a heater is as long as it does the job. This, however, would overlook one or two important aspects. If you use a heater that is well beyond the wattage needed to maintain a given temperature, this will mean the thermostat is constantly working and the heater is switching on and off almost nonstop. Conversely, if the heater is barely powerful enough, it will be on almost nonstop, which is hardly to be recommended in terms of its expected life.

Again, if the heater is too powerful and the thermostat breaks down or sticks, the heater will perform to its full capacity and probably cook the fish! Other factors that will influence the choice of heater will be in relation to matters up too much. This may complicate matters when an undergravel biological filter is used. In the event they fail to operate, the whole tank must be stripped down to effect a repair or a replacement. This alone would make them unpopular with most aquarists. This type is rare.

of heat loss. A tank with no glass cover or hood will lose a great deal of heat at the air/water interface. A tank in a room that is unheated for long faster than those that are not.

The most important of all factors will be the size of the aquarium. A 23-gallon tank will lose heat at a tremendous

Marine aquarium backgrounds insulate as they decorate.

periods of time will also need a more powerful heater than one that is constantly heated to a higher temperature. The differential between the room and aquarium temperatures will thus be much smaller. Tanks exposed to drafts will lose heat rate compared to a 55-gallon unit, which will lose it faster than an 80-gallon tank, and so on. Given all of these variable considerations, I would suggest that you rely greatly on your dealer's advice.

When purchasing heaters you should

figure on using more watts per gallon for smaller tanks. A 29-gallon tank could use 5 watts per gallon, but a larger tank only 3 watts per gallon. A 55-gallon tank would thus utilize one heater becomes jammed in the "on" position, its effect will be minimized because the other will cut out once the water has reached the required temperature.

Tank Capacity (US Gal)	Watts Per Gallon	Total Wattage
29	5	150
40	4-5	175
55	4	200
75	3	225
Over 75	3	Variable

150 or 200 watts. The recommendations quoted are thus flexible and are purely a starting guide. It is always better to obtain two (or more) heaters to produce your wattage than one, depending on tank size. This provides you with extra safety. If one heater fails, the tank will be very slow to lose its heat because the other will no doubt still be functioning. If

HEATER-THERMOSTAT OPTIONS

The first thing that should be said is that modern heaters and thermostats are both relatively inexpensive and efficient. There is quite an extensive variety for you to choose from and, as always, you should think in terms of buying the best you can afford. Your major choice will be between fully

High-intensity spotlights give off heat as well as light. They can be attached to a thermostat to turn them on and off if the tank overheats.

submersible models and those that are not fully submersible. In times past a choice commonly also would have had to be made between obtaining a heater and a separate heater/ thermostat combined into one unit. Today the latter are seen only rarely.

The most popular models are the fully submersible combination units, as these can more easily be hidden behind rocks or other decorations. Many are pre-set at the factory to 24°C (75°F), which happens to be a very popular temperature for both marine and freshwater tropical fishes. Semi-submersibles can often have the temperature altered via a dial on their top. With submersibles the temperature-altering mechanism can vary from brand to brand, so dangerous to you combination. Don't play around and do a lot of experimenting when you have your hands in the tank and the equipment is plugged in.

It is always advisable to ensure that your

The Spotted Snake Eel, *Ophichthys ophis*, from Bonaire.

hang onto the directions that come with the heater until you've amassed some experience with the unit. And at this point it's worth while to reinforce the idea that electricity and water make a bad–that is, heater is fitted with a pilot light to indicate when it is on. Make occasional checks to see whether the pilot light is operating properly.

If two heaters are being used, they should be placed at opposite ends of the tank to ensure an even distribution of heat. The sensors (if micro-chip) or thermostat (if not) are placed away from the heaters, otherwise the heat sensor will react to the local water around the heater rather than that farther away. If two heaters are coupled to a single thermostat, the latter should have a current rating that is slightly in excess of the total of the two heaters–if not its wires will overheat.

Heaters are usually made to be placed in the

The most popular aquarium heaters are those in which the thermostat is built in. Before you put the heater into your marine aquarium, be sure that the water is at room temperature.

upright position, some having suction pads so that they can be attached to a tank side. There are some models that are constructed so that they can be operated in the horizontal position. Follow the recommendations of the manufacturer on this aspect. No glass heaters should ever be placed into the gravel, as this will cause local overheating of the glass, which may then shatter, or at least crack and render it unsafe. Never lift a heater out of the aquarium while it is switched on. Apart from the risk of getting a very bad burn, you will more than likely break the heater. The glass will quickly overheat in contact with air and may shatter or crack.

Bear these facts in mind when making partial or total water changes. If cold water is poured into the tank and onto a working heater,

this will result in disproportionate cooling of the glass, which will probably shatter. These are very delicate precision appliances and must be treated with the utmost care. A number of the micro-chip thermostats come complete with brackets by which they can be hung in the tank. They are claimed to be stainless steel, but nonetheless I would be inclined to sheath them in rubber, mount them onto the glass with double sided sticky tape, or lay them on a nearby surface. This overcomes any risk of the salt water corroding the metal. All appliances with metal components open to the air are at risk near a marine aquarium, and no metal clips should ever be placed into the tank itself.

A final point on heaters is that you may be able to purchase thermofilter units. In these, the water is heated as it passes

through the filter. Their value may one day be proven and there will be one less appliance to place into the display aquarium.

When you purchase your heaters you should test them to see whether they will achieve what is required of them before you actually use them to heat an aquarium in which fishes are residing. This would normally be at the time you set the tank up, as this should precede the arrival of the fishes by several days. In this way, if

Most thermostatically controlled heaters have an ON-light by which the unit can be set. Attach the heater-thermostat to the tank and give it an hour or two to acclimate to the tank's temperature. Then turn the dial until the light goes on. Wait another hour; check the temperature. Keep this up until the tank reaches the proper temperature.

the heater fails or proves to be underpowered, you can adjust matters. It is also wise to keep a spare heater on hand just in case it is needed.

THERMOMETERS

Although heater thermostats are generally very reliable, it is prudent to include one or two thermometers in your aquarium system. These more readily tell you that the water is at the desired temperature or whether it is not. Thermostats can fail to operate for one reason or another. You should make a habit of checking the temperature every time you view the aquarium.

Thermometers come in various forms, some being internal to the tank and others being external, i.e., liquid crystal strips stuck to the side of the tank. The internal models may be filled with mercury or alcohol; the alcohol types are recommended.

Some heaters even have a built-in thermometer.

Although it is unlikely that the thermometer will break, if it did and it was of the mercury type, this could endanger the fishes. You can also obtain combined thermometer/hydrometers. You should place thermometers at opposite ends of the tank, one low in the water and one high up so that you can adjust the equipment to overcome layering.

Stratification, or layering, of the water in an aquarium can be a problem in deep tanks especially. Fortunately, the problem is easily solved simply by increasing circulation in the tank.

Penn-Plax makes two-sided backgrounds for marine aquariums. There may even be some which change with the temperature of the aquarium water.

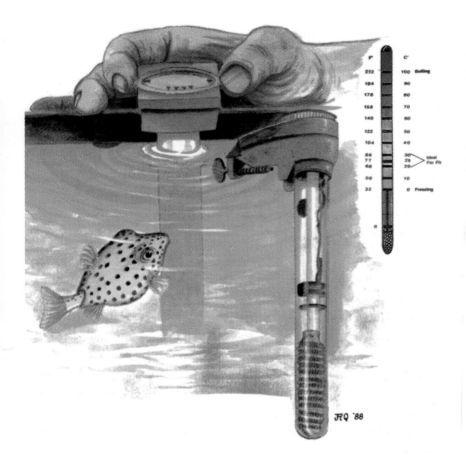

Many aquarium heaters feature calibrated top adjustments for temperature control. These adjustments are relative and not exact. The adjustments must be calibrated with an aquarium thermometer.

Aeration and Filtration

The objectives of the aeration and filtration processes are to both oxygenate and cleanse the water in your aquarium. In this way it can be recirculated, thus used many times before there is a need to replace portions of it. If you did not aerate and filter your tank water, it would quickly become a smelly and lethal body of water. It would be murky and in such a condition that nothing but dangerous bacteria could live in it.

Although filtration systems can seem complex to the first time fishkeeper, this is not the case if you take a simplified view of what is happening. The basis of all filter systems is the same, whether they be low cost or the latest high tech "total" water purification systems that are extremely complex and costly. The differences between them are related to the amount of purification that is taking place.

If you have a volume of water in which there are pieces of visible debris, you can remove these by passing the water through a mesh in which the hole size is smaller than the debris particles. Only the very tiniest pieces of dirt will then be left in the water. If you then passed the water through an even finer material, even less debris would be left, and the water would look a lot cleaner. This type of filtration is called mechanical filtration, for it merely strains out visible detritus by passing it through a mechanical barrier. Periodically, you can remove the filter material and clean or replace it. Many materials can be used as mechanical filters–nylon wool, charcoal, filter pads, nylon brushes, gravel, and even special glass chips. In very large aquariums and in ponds, settlement tanks are used, so the dirt can sink to the bottom and be drained off; this may be regarded as prefiltration.

Mechanical filtration does not, however, remove chemicals and gases that are in a dissolved state. To achieve this the water must pass through a material, such as charcoal, that will cause the chemicals to adhere to the surfaces of the grains. This type of filtration is known as chemical filtration. Most chemical filters will also

Today's filters and filter media have advanced to the point that marine aquariums can be kept crystal clear.

act as mechanical filters because they will impede the progress of debris. The charcoal to be used is of a special type that has been "activated" by being heated to a high degree so that tiny pores are opened in it. Normal charcoal is unsuitable.

Even after water has been treated by both mechanical and chemical means, there will still be toxic chemicals that have not been removed. Some of these, such as the gases chlorine and carbon dioxide, will dissipate into the atmosphere if the water from the lower levels is constantly brought to the surface. Yet others provide food for plants, but in the average

Aquarium shops feature very sophisticated and efficient high-volume filters. Visit your pet shop and discuss your needs with a knowledgeable salesperson.

home marine aquarium
these will not normally
be present in significant
quantities. However,
before they are
converted by plants into
food they must be
changed from their
original dangerous state
to a less toxic form: this
is done by the action of
certain beneficial
bacteria. These
organisms live on rocks,
gravel, sand, and in fact
most surfaces. They are
aerobic, thus need
plenty of oxygen to
survive and build up
colonies. Along with
plants, they constitute
examples of what is
called biological
filtration.

By the time the water
has been subjected to
these various filters it is
on its way to becoming
very clean and quite
suitable for sustaining
fishes. It may, however,
still contain harmful
bacteria that could
cause diseases in the
fishes. If you wanted to
remove most of these

Many marine animals, fishes and invertebrates included, are scavengers and help in keeping the tank clean, but they all excrete waste products, so don't overload your aquarium.

you could pass the water through yet other items, such as ozonizers and ultraviolet sterilizers, which would kill most of them off. By now the water would be both crystal clear and free from most things you would not want in it. Such appliances are called purification or sterilization filters. The water resulting from these might even be too sterile in the view of some enthusiasts.

What you now need is some means of pushing the water through these various filters, and this is done with a pump. The latter may simply be an air line, or, more commonly, a pump built into the filter system so that it draws water through the filter material at a faster rate. In a well filtered aquarium the entire volume of water may pass through the filter chambers in a relatively short time. The filter system could be placed in sealed units within the aquarium, but it would take up a lot of space and make cleaning difficult. It is therefore normally placed near the tank, but discreetly hidden in a tank stand or similar place.

AERATION

The amount of oxygen any body of water contains is determined to a large degree by its surface area, for this is where the oxygen is dissolved. Seas and oceans have enormous surface areas and can sustain billions of life forms. The carbon dioxide released by the fishes and other aerobic organisms, plus that from plants, is dissipated from the water at its surface. You will therefore appreciate how important a good surface area is (and why tall narrow tanks create problems). The oxygen-rich surface water is taken to the lower depths by currents. Storms and tides agitate the water, which effectively increases the latter's surface area, allowing the maximum amount of oxygen to be dissolved in it.

In the aquarium you can create miniature waves by disturb-ing the water surface in some way. This can be done

Myrichthys acuminatus is not a fish for beginners.

by sending up a stream of bubbles from an air stone placed at the bottom of the tank, or by returning the filtered water so that it sprays onto the surface–or you could do both. Aquarists often increase the oxygen content by means of the filter system, so when power filters are fitted there is no real need to use air stones.

Although you will see them in aquariums fitted with power filters, this is usually done in order to create a curtain of bubbles, which can look attractive. Please note that increased oxygen created by air stones is the result of the agitation of the water surface, not because the air bubbles themselves contribute to the supply. Most bubbles do not burst until they reach the surface, so they are more visual rather than actual contributors in themselves.

If you decide to feature an independent aeration system in your aquarium, you can purchase an inexpensive diaphragm pump, to which you can connect one or more plastic airlines. These are then attached to any of the many air stones or similar diffusers that your local aquarium store will stock. They are then placed at the rear of the tank, or even in artificial rocks, so as to create an interesting effect. Be sure to fit one-way valves into the air lines so that in the event the pump should fail, the water will not back-siphon into the pump, to no doubt ruin it and perhaps empty the tank of water as well. Some diaphragm pumps tend to "wander" on smooth surfaces because of their vibration, so it may be best to suspend them, which will also help to reduce any vibration noise they may produce.

FILTER SYSTEMS

If you have understood the foregoing review of aeration and filtration, then you will appreciate the differences in the systems we will now consider for your aquarium. I should first state that you should not be unduly concerned about the cost of, or any need to use, purification filters. These are not essential to your aquarium, even less so if you will not risk

An outside power filter.

overloading your filter system by trying to keep too many fishes in the one tank. You may be told that by having good aeration and filtration you can increase the number of fishes the water will be capable of sustaining. This is true, but there is a down side to it. If the filtration system should fail, the overstocked water will quickly deteriorate and you will have real problems on your hands. Filtration merely ensures better water conditions for your fishes, thus less risk of health problems. It should not be used as a means of increasing the tank's stock levels beyond a reasonable degree.

EXTERNAL CANISTER FILTERS

A very popular filter used by aquarists is the external power canister filter. This tall cylinder is fitted with

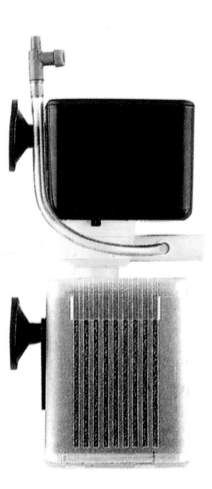

Powerful sponge filters are excellent for additional filtering but are not for everyday duty in a marine aquarium.

an electric impeller that draws water from the aquarium into the base of the canister. The water is then pumped through differing filter media, such as nylon floss, special ceramic or glass chips, charcoal, or even compressed nylon pot scourers. It is then returned to the aquarium via a spray bar or other head. This agitates the water surface to increase the latter's oxygen-dissolving potential.

The filter must be left running continually and must be cleaned on a regular basis. If this is not attended to the filter media will become saturated and thereafter will allow toxic dissolved gases to pass through the system and be returned to the aquarium water. If there is ever a need to add medicines to

Canister filters, available at your aquarium shop, are very useful with the marine aquarium because of their ability to create water currents.

the water, it is essential that chemical filters, such as activated charcoal, are removed. If they are not they will adsorb the medicines, and thus neutralize their benefits. The mechanical filters in the canister provide, as a bonus, a limited degree of biological filtration, provided you do not kill the beneficial bacteria by washing the filter material in hot water.

UNDERGRAVEL FILTERS

One of the reasons marine aquarists have been more successful in the last decade is because the use of biological filters has become much more popular. This is a very natural form of filtration: it has even become a favorite with those wanting really clean garden ponds. Decomposed food, together with fecal matter from the fishes, is rich in ammonia and its compounds (such as nitrites). These are potentially lethal to the fishes if present beyond only a small level. In the ocean they are not a problem, because the volume of water is so large that it dilutes them to a non-

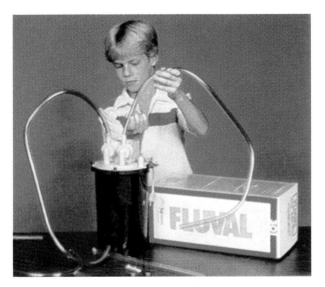

There is nothing complicated about a canister filter, but get instructions from your supplier concerning starting it.

problematic level. Furthermore, the enormous quantities of plankton and kelp and other algae utilize nitrates as food. Nitrates are a less lethal form of nitrites. They are produced by the action of aerobic (oxygen utilizing) bacteria that live on rocks, on the ocean bed, and even on plant matter itself.

In order to survive, the bacteria that convert nitrites to nitrates need lots of oxygen. If the latter is in short supply, then the beneficial bacteria start to die, and nitrates are converted back into nitrites. This creates a dangerous negative cycle.

The undergravel filter is composed of a plastic plate in which there are numerous holes. Its edges raise the plate just above the floor of the aquarium. An uplift tube is fitted from one, or even better two, of the corners. The substrate of the aquarium is then placed over the plate. Water is drawn down through the substrate either by air from a pump or by a power head fitted to the uplift tube(s). The substrate is thus provided with a constant supply of oxygen-rich water so that it is able to sustain a very large colony of beneficial bacteria.

The system just described is known as a down-flow system, because the water is taken downward and returned at the surface. Its singular drawback is that it tends to clog the substrate with debris, which obviously places more of a workload on the beneficial bacteria.

The photos below and on the facing page show some Dupla equipment based upon biological filtration principles. Very expensive systems and complex systems are available.

A beautiful Dupla-controlled marine aquarium.

This can be overcome by regular cleaning of the substrate or by using a reverse, or up-flow, system. The reverse flow system works by having the water taken from just above the substrate (where it is dirtiest) and passed through a power canister filter or similar appliance. The water is thus precleaned and then sent down the uplift tube and under the filter plate. It then passes upward through the substrate, providing this with clean oxygen-laden water.

If the up-flow system has a drawback, it lies in the fact that it does not maximize the potential oxygen content of the water. This being so, additional aeration is beneficial. It may also keep detritus in suspension just above the substrate, which is why it is useful to take the water from this area to the external power filter for cleansing.

ALGAL FILTERS

Marine aquariums do not always feature aquatic plants, yet these provide many benefits to the water purification process. They absorb chemicals as well as carbon dioxide. One way to utilize their benefits is to pass the water in the aquarium through an algal filter. The latter consists of one or more trays of coral gravel or sand that are subjected to bright light. This encourages surface algae to grow much more robustly than might be desired in the aquarium. The water is sprayed over the surface algae; it filters down through the substrate and is then returned to the aquarium.

Biological filtration depends on bacteria growing on exposed surfaces. The greater the surface, the more bacteria, thus the more efficiency. Various "surfaces" are available at your pet shop.

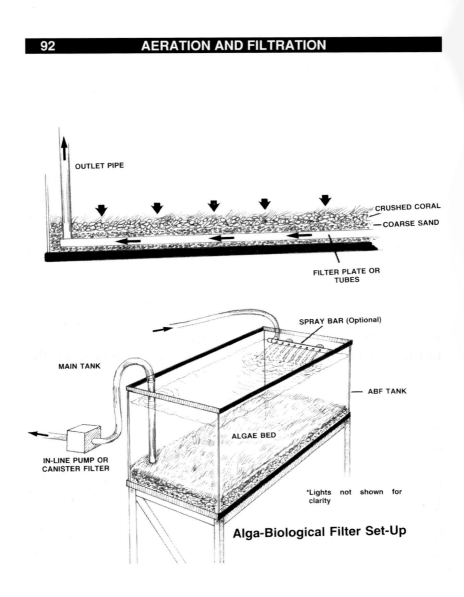

OUTLET PIPE

CRUSHED CORAL

COARSE SAND

FILTER PLATE OR TUBES

SPRAY BAR (Optional)

MAIN TANK

ABF TANK

ALGAE BED

IN-LINE PUMP OR CANISTER FILTER

*Lights not shown for clarity

Alga-Biological Filter Set-Up

Algae are immensely helpful in an aquarium. They absorb heavy metals, produce oxygen, absorb carbon dioxide, and are pleasant to look at when they grow densely and in beds. Of course, this only occurs in the presence of strong light. Using these facts, biological algae filters have been designed.

EXTERNAL BIOLOGICAL FITERS

If an undergravel filter should become clogged with dirt over a period of time (possibly because it is working less than efficiently), this can result in the aquarist having to strip the aquarium down in order to clean it. This disturbs the whole ecosystem and may dramatically reduce the size of the bacterial colony. To overcome this possibility, the biological filter can be accommodated in a second tank. The benefits are that it becomes possible to clean the filter without disturbing the show tank. At the same time, the undergravel filter can be placed in a larger tank than the display unit, thus offering better filtration. Alternatively, the beneficial bacteria can be encouraged to colonize trays. These can be placed horizontally or vertically in the second aquarium.

Chaetodon paucifasciatus. This and other many other butterflyfish species present feeding difficulties.

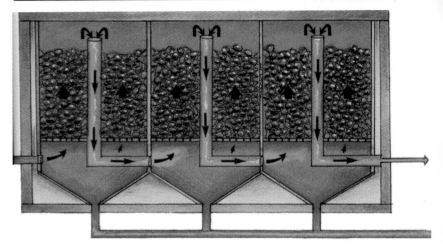

External heavy-duty biological filters are based upon a huge amount of surfaces upon which the bacteria grow. This triple unit biological filter passes water through three beds of irregularly shaped gravel.

There are in fact no limitations to the ways you could devise to filter the aquarium water. Filter brushes made from nylon are available in numerous sizes, and these can be placed into special filter chambers of external units. They will house large colonies of nitrifying bacteria and can be periodically cleansed in a rotational manner so that there is always a good colony left in the chamber. Wet/dry filter systems are used by aquarists having large setups and the space to house the filter trays in concealed cabinets. Such systems pass the water over trays of gravel that are raised above the water of the filter chamber. It then percolates through the trays and finally falls into the wet part of the system for final filtration before being returned to the aquarium. The water may even be passed through a chamber containing bio-balls. These are small polyethylene balls of varying sizes that increase greatly the surface area the water passes over; in so doing the water is aerated considerably.

The chosen filter system will clearly reflect the size of the aquarium you have purchased. If you keep the stocking level well within the capacity of the water volume, there will be minimal strain on the filter system, so further filtration processes will not be necessary. However, with some units the aquarist may be concerned about the risk of parasites, so other systems have been devised that will largely overcome the risk associated with these.

ULTRAVIOLET LIGHT STERILIZATION

Ultraviolet light kills most bacteria (including those that are beneficial), so the use of such equipment should be subject to caution and is not without associated problems. The

The triple unit shown on the facing page has a shortcoming. The heavy matter may clog up the water passage through the gravel. By using settling tanks, the heavy particles fall to the bottom and can be mechanically drained, thereby keeping the gravel free of coarse material.

ultraviolet lamp is concealed in a casing of quartz, which in turn is contained in a protective sheath. Water is passed into the sheath and is subjected to the U-V rays. The success of the UV lamp is subject to certain requirements. The water should already be clean, so that the U-V rays do not bombard dirt, which would reduce the efficiency of the lamp. The flow rate of the water should be slow enough for maximum exposure to the rays. The lamp is placed in an external position and has its own starter switch so that you can control the extent of sterilization. The life of a UV lamp, like fluorescent lighting, is limited, even though it may still appear to be working. Follow the manufacturer's recommendations on the use and life of the

Aquarium shops usually carry UV sterilizers. They can be dangerous. Read the instructions carefully and get further instruction from the source from whom you purchased the units.

lamp. If fishes have been living in water that has been UV treated for long periods, it may considerably reduce their ability to ward off pathogenic organisms. If they are transferred to "normal" aquarium water, they may quickly succumb to bacterial attack. In order to resist a disease, an organism builds up immunity by being exposed to low level bacterial presence. If this is removed, as with the use of UV lamps, so is the immunity, thus very advanced sterilization equipment is not always favored by aquarists seeking to develop natural systems.

PROTEIN SKIMMERS

Protein skimmers are also referred to as air strippers or foam fractionators. They are used in marine aquariums to cause protein molecules (such as from uneaten food and other decaying matter) to be subjected to a stream of air bubbles. This results in the molecules being deposited at a suitable water surface in the form of a frothy foam where it can then be removed. Even in an aquarium that has water that looks very clean and clear there are many invisible and detrimental organic compounds that only a skimmer will remove effectively. In fact, it is possible to run a marine tank with a skimmer as the only filter. At any rate, a skimmer is always a help in maintaining water quality. Protein skimmers will not remove detritus that is heavier than water, as this will sink to the substrate.

There are three types of protein skimmer available. One is called the direct current type, another is the countercurrent model, and the last is the venturi skimmer. In the direct current models an air stone is fitted within a large air-lift tube. At the top of this a chamber prevents the accumul-ated foam from being recircul-ated into the tank

Sponge filters are very helpful in controlling occasional blooms of algae or cloudy water.

water. The protein molecules cling to the rising air bubbles. However, because the water flow tends to be quite fast, this limits the effectiveness of the direct current skimmer. In the counter-current models the water is circulated in the opposite direction to the rising air bubbles, which slows down the

flow rate and thus increases the time the water is exposed to the bubbles. In venturi skimmers a water pump creates a swirling vortex, increasing contact time between bubbles and water even more.

Very often, the air in the main tube has been passed through an ozonizer, which both kills bacteria and aerates the water. Excess ozone (O_3) is dangerous to fishes (and to humans), so water that contains it should be passed through a carbon filter which will remove the extra molecule of oxygen. The use of an ozonizer in an aquarium setup carries many dangers, as it will

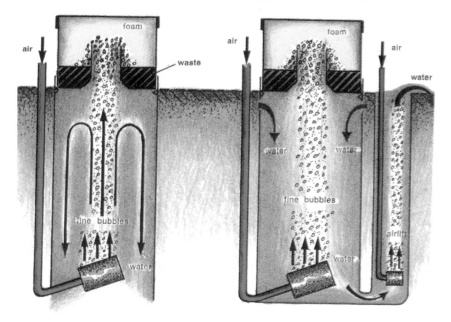

Two designs for popular protein skimmers. Your local aquarium supplier has units made to fit tanks of various sizes.

break down vitamins as well as decaying proteins. It can result in burns to the fishes if it is allowed to enter the aquarium water. The beginner is advised not to use high tech equipment (UV sterilizers and complex protein skimmers utilizing ozone) unless professional advice is provided in setting up the installation. Even then it must be monitored very carefully, as excess ozone will cause valves to become brittle and rubber connections will be badly damaged.

It is always best to discuss very advanced filtration systems with your dealer first. They are invariably not needed if your aquarium is well balanced and not overstocked. It is always better to try and

keep things as simple–
thus as natural–as
possible when keeping
any form of fish. If you
have a problem with your
aquarium, discuss the
matter with your dealer
or a known expert. They
may pinpoint the source,
which may not require
investment in complex
equipment to overcome
it. Very often, beginners
invest in state-of-the-art
systems because they
think these are essential,
or simply so that they
have them. Such
equipment necessitates a
very sound knowledge of
the chemical reactions
that they employ, which
the novice rarely has
until practical experience
has been gained a little
at a time.

A juvenile specimen of *Pomacanthus imperator*. Like many other marine
fishes, this species undergoes striking changes in its colors and color pattern
as it matures.

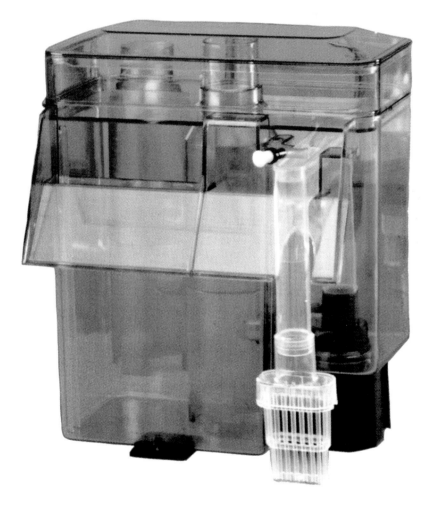

A modern external filter in which a protein skimmer is installed is called a "Skilter" TM.

Above: *Pomacanthus arcuatus*. Below: *Holacanthus ciliaris*.

Properties of Water

In order to increase the chances that your fishes will survive it is essential that basic water chemistry is understood at least sufficiently that certain tests can be made on the aquarium water. The most obvious difference between fresh and sea water is the fact that the latter contains salt. Fishes adapted to living in fresh water cannot survive in sea water, though some species are able to cope with brackish water. Freshwater fishes have body fluids that are more dense than the waters in which they live. As a result, water is continually passing inward through their

Scats (*Scatophagus argus* shown here) and monos are the most common representatives in the aquarium trade of fish that are comfortable in fresh, brackish, and full salt water.

skin by a process called osmosis. The fish must continually lose water via their urine otherwise they would literally burst. They also drink very little water.

Marine fishes have the reverse problem. The water in which they live has a higher concent-

Measuring the density of salt water with a hydrometer.

ration of salts than their body fluids. They continually lose water to their environment. To overcome this they drink copious amounts of water and minimize the water lost through urination.

SPECIFIC GRAVITY (RELATIVE DENSITY)

The amount of salts in any volume of liquid is expressed by a comparison to that of distilled water, via their respective densities. Distilled water has a specific gravity (density) of 1, so that any liquid with a density above this may be regarded as saline. The degree of such salinity will of course be determined by its specific gravity. The latter can be expressed as such, or as grams per liter (gm/liter). Temperature is also an important consideration, because the higher the temperature, the lower the SG of a liquid. With this in mind, it is recommended that the marine aquarist work within a range of a specific gravity of 1.020-

1.025 at a temperature of 78-80°F (25-26.5°C). The lower end of this SG range is somewhat lower than that found in the various oceans of the world, but it will place less strain on the fishes in terms of their coping with their water loss. However, you should endeavor to match the SG of the water to that of the environment (ocean) where the fish would normally be found. For example, most marine fishes are taken from the Indian, Pacific, and Atlantic Oceans, which have SG values in the range of 1.022-1.026. The Red Sea, on the other hand, has a SG of around 1.030.

You can determine the specific gravity by use of a hydrometer. This can either be of the floating type or one that is filled with a sample of the water. The latter indicates the SG via a pointer/needle. It is important that the hydrometer is calibrated to the approximate temperature range you are working with, otherwise an incorrect reading will be obtained. It is wise to take regular readings of the SG because water is constantly being lost through evaporation. This will result in a greater concentration of salts, which do not evaporate, thus raising the SG. Fresh water (at the correct temperature) must then be added in order to maintain the desired SG. Checks should be made about every other week. Weekly checks are advised where small aquariums are kept, because the smaller the unit, the more rapidly the water properties can change.

THE pH OF THE WATER

The pH is a measure of acidity or alkalinity. It is expressed on a scale of 0-14, with 7

The hydrometer floats in the water to be tested. The level at which it floats is calibrated. The reading of normal aquarium salt water is 1.022 to 1.026 as shown above.

being regarded as the neutral point. Water above pH 7 is alkaline, that below it is acidic. Marine fishes prefer alkaline waters that have a pH in the range 8-8.3. This may not seem much of a range, but if it is remembered that water at 8 is ten times more alkaline than that at 7, it can be seen that water at 8.3 is considerably more alkaline than that at 8. Marine fishes will not do well if the pH drops below this latter value.

The pH can easily be measured using one of the numerous test kits that all pet and aquatic stores sell. They operate by adding a sample of the tank water to a container, adding the supplied reagent, and comparing the result to a color chart that comes with the kit. In order to ensure that a correct reading is made, the color chart should be kept in a darkened place (in the test kit box). If it is subjected to light for any length of time it will of course become faded. You can also purchase an electronic pH meter, but these are rather expensive.

The pH value of aquarium water will change as it ages. In the marine aquarium it will tend to become more acidic as a result of carbon dioxide in the water and the breakdown of organic matter. To overcome this problem, partial water changes (about 10%) once a week will help maintain the needed value. Alternatively, sodium bicarbonate can be added to the water (1/2 teaspoon per 100 liters) and this will maintain the buffer capacity of the water. The latter is the term used to indicate a water's capacity to resist changes to its pH value. However, if chemical buffer strengtheners are used in the absence of water changes, they can lead to a build-up of unwanted chemicals, so partial water changes are normally the best way to maintain pH values. It can be added that the addition of calcareous (calcium-containing) rocks, such as chalk, marble, and the like, does not actually stabilize the pH to any great degree as has generally been assumed for years in aquaculture.

AMMONIA AND ITS COMPOUNDS

Ammonia (NH_3) is a highly poisonous gas that will readily dissolve in water. Even in small amounts it can prove fatal to fishes, for it destroys the delicate mucous membrane of the skin and then penetrates the internal tissues. It is created as a result of the breakdown of nitrogenous products such as fecal matter and proteins. When it combines with water it produces ammonium (NH_4+), which is less harmful but, for marine fishes, is still potentially lethal. This is because the pH value influences the amount of ammonia that a volume of water contains. At low pH values most of the ammonia will be converted to ammonium, but at higher pH values (above 7) this does not happen; in fact it increases the ammonia levels.

At a pH of 8 there is too much ammonia present at the water temperature most marine fish are kept in–more than enough to kill all the fishes in an aquarium. If the temperature rises, so does the amount of ammonia. This relationship between toxic ammonia and pH is an important reason why the marine hobbyist has more problems than does the freshwater aquarist, because below a pH of 7 all the ammonia is converted to ammonium.

Ammonia is utilized by certain plant life as a form of food, and it is also a food to anaerobic (non oxygen-breathing) organisms. These bacteria (*Nitrosomonas*) convert ammonia to nitrite (NO_2-), which is only a little less harmful than ammonia. However, other bacteria (*Nitrobacter*) convert nitrite into nitrate (NO_3-). This can be tolerated much better by the fishes

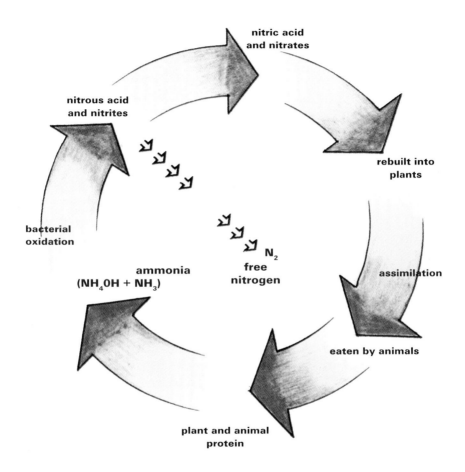

The nitrogen cycle demonstrates what occurs when the wastes of assimilation (the incorporation of food by plants and animals) are converted by bacterial oxidation to nitrogenous compounds.

(but far less so by many invertebrates and anemones), and is utilized by plants (usually algae in marine tanks) as a food source.

Nitrobacter are aerobic bacteria that live on the substrate; it takes them time to form colonies in aquariums. This is why the newly set up unit is the one most likely to suffer from ammonia or nitrite poisoning. Once biological filters are working they will (or should) remove ammonia and nitrites. This assumes, however, that the aquarium is not overstocked, the fish not overfed, and that regular partial water changes are taking place.

You can test for ammonia, nitrite, and nitrate levels using one of the test kits from your local supplier. These come with complete instructions. After the initial maturation period the ammonia and nitrite levels should be at zero, or very near zero. The nitrate level should not be allowed to become excessive, though this is unlikely if partial water changes are routine and general management is sound. Remember that the ammonia-nitrite-nitrate cycle is reversible. By this is meant that if the filter system is not operating efficiently, then nitrate will be converted to nitrite, and this to ammonia, thus putting in motion a negative cycle.

If an ozonizer is part of a marine setup, this will also remove nitrite. The unstable extra oxygen atom of ozone (O_3) will readily attach itself to the nitrogen atoms of the nitrite molecule (NO_2-) to form nitrate (NO_3-). However, the negative aspect is that once all of the nitrite is converted to nitrate, the ozone may burn the skin of the fish unless the water is passed through a carbon filter.

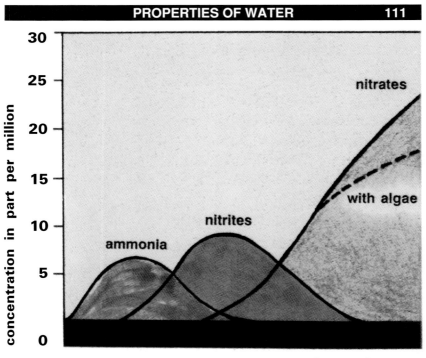

The conversion of ammonia to nitrites and eventually to relatively harmless nitrates is a function of time.

CARBON DIOXIDE

Carbon dioxide (CO_2) is a byproduct of fishes' and other life forms' respiration. It dissolves in water to form carbonic acid (H_2CO_3). It is also dissipated into the atmosphere at the water surface. Good water circulation will prevent any buildup of this gas, and regular partial water changes will ensure that the carbonic acid does not reduce the pH value such that this results in a buildup of ammonia.

OXYGEN

Oxygen is, of course, vital to both the fishes and other organisms in a marine tank. If it is in short supply the fishes will be seen to hang just beneath the water

Centropyge flavissimus in its natural habitat.

surface gasping for air. The beneficial bacteria needed in the nitrogen cycle will obviously be affected; thus biological filtration will deteriorate. The usual cause of oxygen starvation is overstocking the tank, coupled with a rise in water temperature (the higher the temperature, the less oxygen it can dissolve). The remedy is to aerate the tank rapidly to overcome the short-term needs of the fishes, then to either purchase a larger aquarium or reduce the number of fishes being accommodated.

Oxygen super-saturation is the result of excess oxygen and is manifested by the formation of tiny bubbles on the rocks and other decorations. It may result in gas embolism, which may be seen as a bubble in the eye of a fish. It is often the result of excessive algal growth, excess light, and low stocking levels. The answer is to rapidly aerate the water, which will allow the surplus oxygen to escape, then to reduce the light level, which will slow down the rate of algal growth.

Fishes from less than truly tropical waters in general have greater oxygen requirements than those from really warmwater areas; the Porkfish, *Anisotremus virginicus*, is an example.

Your aquarium shop will have various testing kits to assist you in the control of ammonia, copper, nitrites, and other dangerous substances.

Adequate ventilation to the aquarium is essential to allow all excess gases to escape. Oxygen supersaturation is not normally a problem, so the beginner should not worry about it, but simply be aware of it.

CHLORINE

Chlorine is a poisonous gas; it is also a very common additive to the domestic water supply as a means of killing potentially harmful bacteria. It is easily removed by vigorous aeration of the water prior to its being used to prepare the salt water. However, more and more water authorities are using chloramine these days, which is more stable than chlorine and therefore not removable by simple aeration. You can purchase water de-chlorinators that also remove chloramine; these are recommended as a way to prepare the water.

COPPER

Copper and its many compound forms, such as copper sulfate, are highly toxic to fishes, yet copper is the basic element in many treatments for aquarium fishes. In years past its use was on a rather hit and miss basis–the miss meaning an overdose that killed the patient! Today you can purchase test kits that measure the copper content of the water. These are recommended in the event medicines based on this metal are used. It is also advisable, when preparing aquarium water, to run the faucet for a few seconds. This is especially necessary if you have been on vacation, because the water in the pipes, if they are made of copper, may contain higher than desirable levels of this metal. It is best to treat ailing fishes in an isolation tank, this being especially wise with copper treatments.

In the foregoing review of water properties, the minimum of information has been supplied with respect to the chemical processes that take place. There is in fact no limit to the amount of studying an enthusiast could undertake on this subject. It must be stressed that marine fishes are not comparable to goldfish and other hardy species which you may have kept at some time in your life. They must have a stable environment in which to live. This environment must be clean and maintained on a very regular basis. It is not possible to ignore the water conditions for weeks and then try to correct problems during one hectic rush of activity. This will stress the fishes badly: if they are not already past saving this could be the final straw. Take regular water samples and test them for those items discussed. Make regular partial water changes, do not overstock the aquarium, and never overfeed the fishes. Clean filters as needed. Always remember that the marine aquarium is a far cry from the oceans in which your fishes probably originated. You cannot hope to duplicate their environment, but with constant attention to general water husbandry you may be able to provide them with a miniature world that enables them to survive. The longer they live, the greater the compliment to your understanding of their needs.

Chaetodon ocellatus is especially sensitive to heavy-metal poisoning.

Setting Up the Aquarium

Under this heading is also included consideration of the tank decorations, which can obviously vary from the very simple to the highly ornate.

The beginner is advised to try and keep things relatively simple. By so doing it allows experience to be gained a little at a time, without the added complications to water chemistry that may result if decorations are not chosen wisely, or have not been cleansed sufficiently. In any case, it allows more room for the fish to swim in–an important aspect if the initial aquarium is of only a small to moderate size.

DECORATIVE MATERIALS

The materials that form the tank decoration comprise everything in the aquarium other than the equipment. This will mean the substrate (the bottom covering), rocks, corals, plants, and any novelty items

Colored gravel is not indicated for a marine tank. The red gravel was used for photographic purposes only.

(such as treasure chests and their like). Novelty items are not popular with marine aquarists. It is recommended that the beginner not commence with living coral because it is not only expensive, but difficult to maintain. Likewise, the only plants that the novice might try will be species of algae that have a higher plant look to them. However, even these will require special attention with respect to their lighting and other needs. This being so, the best course is to feature imitation plants if some greenery is desired. Once you are satisfied you can maintain the marine aquarium, you can then experiment a little at a time by trying living plants and corals. Even invertebrates are best left out of the initial aquarium, because they are much more sensitive than the fishes to water properties. They will quickly perish if these change beyond the small levels of fluctuation they can tolerate.

THE SUBSTRATE

The marine hobbyist has more options for selection of the substrate than does the freshwater aquarist.

The undergravel filter is covered over with just the lift tubes protruding from the substrate.

This is because the latter fishkeeper is usually concerned about not increasing the hardness and alkalinity of the water, so calcareous materials are not used. These are not a problem to the marine aquarium, for they can provide an excellent covering for an undergravel filter, if used, and may help a little in stabilizing the pH. The most popular substrate materials will be coral sand and crushed seashell or coral. You can use ordinary aquarium gravel if you wish, but this would not be found on the ocean floor, so if used it is best to cover it with a layer of coral sand so the bottom looks more natural.

You should purchase the substrate material from your local pet or aquatic dealer, rather than taking it from seashores. The problem with these sources is that they may have unwanted organic materials on them. You would have to boil or steam clean the substrate very carefully before using it, so all in all the small cost of purchasing a safe material from your dealer is the best way to proceed.

Two grades of substrate are needed, one fine and one coarse. The coarse grade is placed over the filter plate and provides a vast surface area for the nitrifying bacteria to live on. The finer grade sand (but not too fine) is placed on top of this, with a fine plastic mesh separating the two grades. This will minimize the amount of fine sand that falls into the nooks and crannies of the coarser grade, thus reducing its surface area. The fine sand will also provide a welcome retreat for those fish species that like to either burrow or browse on the aquarium floor; it will also prevent decaying food or organisms from clogging up the coarser gravel.

ROCKS

There is a wide range of rocks that can be used for decorative purposes, as well as to provide hiding places for the more timid fishes. The point to remember is that the rocks should be free of metal. All calcareous rocks, such as dolomite, chalk, marble, or tufa, will be fine, as are slate, sandstone, and granite. Do not mix too many rocks of differing colors together, as this will make the aquascene look very artificial. Color can come via the fishes.

CORAL

Coral is the calcareous skeletal remains of certain types of coelenterates. These are primitive, hollow organisms with tentacles at their anterior end; sea anemones and jellyfishes are also members of this large group of animals. Coral is available in many very attractive shapes, which is their main attraction to the marine enthusiast. Most coral you can purchase will be white; this is because the color-producing organisms that lived on the coral will of course have died and been removed. However, there are red and blue forms available that retain their colors. Select coral with care because some varieties are extremely brittle, others are very convoluted in shape. The latter look fine, but all of those brain-like convolutions are a potential source of trouble. They can trap particles of food that are not easily removed, and thus could create pollution. Bear in mind that although the coral will be white initially, it will steadily become colonized with algae and will turn green unless you periodically clean it.

As with plants, you can of course purchase artificial coral or rock. The advantages of the artificial decorations are that they are not as heavy and there is virtually no risk that they will leach chemicals into the water. Maybe a combination of real rocks and coral, with some that are artificial, might enable you to have the desired shapes you would like. Because of the endangerment of coral reefs, pieces of dead coral are much less available than formerly.

ALGAE

Algae are simple plants that range from the microscopic to the

Everything that goes into the marine tank must be sterilized clean. Then the decorations may safely be positioned in the substrate.

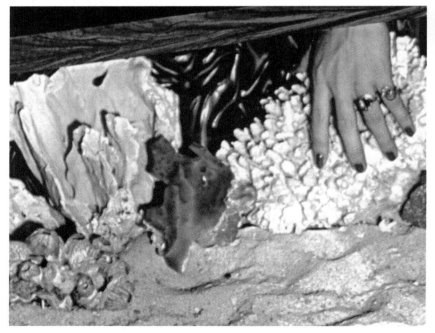

largest plants on our planet–the giant seaweeds (kelp). The bane of freshwater aquarists, green algae are often cultivated by marine hobbyists for their beneficial properties. They utilize nitrates, provide a natural fish food, and add decoration to rocks on which they attach themselves. Good green algal growth is a sign that water conditions are healthy, because these algae cannot survive if water properties are not as the aquarist also wants them to be. If nitrates are in excess of about 20 parts per million (ppm) the algae start to die and may pollute the aquarium, this being their major drawback.

Apart from the filamentous small algae that grow on the glass walls and rocks of the aquarium, there are also more plantlike species. These include species of *Ulva*, *Udotea*, and

especially *Caulerpa*, which offer the enthusiast a number of very interesting shapes. These various species do, however, require quite a lot of light intensity if they are to flourish. See and discuss them with your local pet or aquatic dealer.

There are many species of unwanted algae, such as the brown and the red species, as well as the bluegreen algae (which is not actually a true alga). These types thrive in water that is not generally healthy for the fishes, so they are a sign of poor water conditions. They may often appear when a tank is initially set up but usually die back once the green algae start to colonize the aquarium.

PLANNING THE AQUASCENE

The completed aquarium, with everything in place, is

Even the most simply decorated marine aquarium demands planning.

called the aquascene. It should be planned very carefully, because once the tank is full of water and equipment it is extremely difficult to rearrange. Make a number of drawings of the sort of vista you would like, then purchase whatever is needed to create this. You could even place rocks and equipment (heaters, air stones, tubing) into the aquarium before the water is added so that you can move things around easily to see how they will look. At this stage you do not need to include the substrate. When purchasing coral it is advisable to obtain more than you plan to feature in the aquarium. In this way you can have coral in the tank while the spares are being cleaned.

If your tank is not very large, you may deem it worth considering the

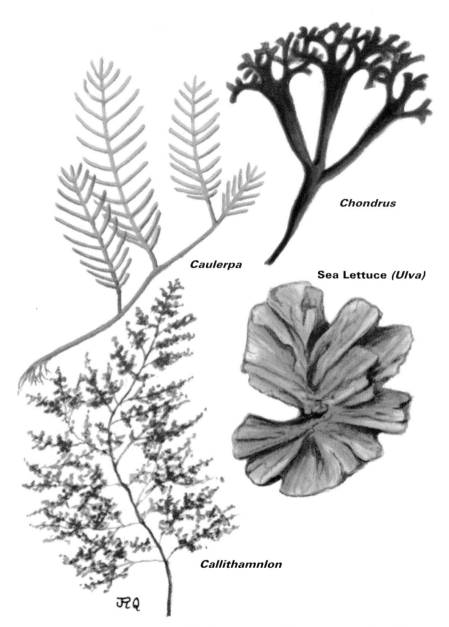

Chondrus

Caulerpa

Sea Lettuce *(Ulva)*

Callithamnlon

Various types of common marine algae

possibility of adding an external "stage" for some of the rocks or coral. This can be placed behind the aquarium. What you do is to make a back lot of wood. This can then be arranged utilizing any of the rocks, corals, and substrates that you wish. The inner walls can be painted a blue-green color, or you might purchase one of the many murals that could be stuck onto the walls of the stage. Some of these are 3-dimensional. Select one that is complementary to the fish species you plan to keep.

If the stage is specifically illuminated with care, the effect is quite surprising. The aquarium seems much larger than it is. The fishes have more swimming area, because some of the larger rocks are on the stage and are not taking up room in the tank. Brittle coral, or that which is very convoluted, may be part of the aquascene without the attendant risk of being broken or polluting the tank as previously discussed. You can also rearrange the stage without interfering with the ecosystem in the tank. If this approach is taken, be sure to remember that you will need extra space on the shelf or whatever is to be the final site of the aquarium to accommodate the stage. You must also consider how you will route the tubing for airstones and filters so that it does not intrude on the scene.

If no back stage is to be used, you should paint, or otherwise cover, the back and side panels of the aquarium. You do not want to see the wallpaper or other wall coverings that are behind the aquarium. Nor do you want to see the filter system or any wires and tubing that may be positioned at the rear of the tank.

An important part of the decor of the marine tank is the background. Decide on the background before you buy and place the decorations in their final position.

CLEANING DECORATIONS

Once you have decided on the aquascene and purchased everything that will be needed for the completed setup, it is then time to clean anything that might be a potential source of harmful organisms being introduced into the aquarium. Substrate, rocks, and corals, regardless of their source, will need an initial cleaning.

Tank: Although most tanks produced these days are very reliable, it would still be prudent to fill the tank with water in order to check that it has no leaks. This should be done outdoors just in case. If a very minor leak is discovered you can repair this using one of the silicone cements from your pet dealer. If there are no leaks you can clean the tank by using a strong saline solution or a commercial aquarium cleaner. Be sure the tank is then fully rinsed. In the case of the disinfectant suggested, the final water to be rinsed out of the tank should be tested for its chlorine content, just to be sure all residual traces have been removed.

Rocks & Coral: These can be cleaned either by being immersed for at least 30 minutes in boiling water or by being placed in a solution of disinfectant. The latter can be obtained from your pet dealer, or you can use a household bleach. *All* traces of such disinfectants must be removed through numerous rinsings with clean water. You could rinse the rocks with a hose, but be careful when using this on coral, as the more delicate varieties could break. After the cleaning process has been completed, the rock or coral can be left to dry in the sun. Just how diligent you are about cleaning should reflect the source of the rock or coral. In the case of the coral, bear in mind that coral is only given a quick cleaning before being shipped from its origin to the dealer. It may still contain the remains of microorganisms trapped in its convolutions. Test the final rinse water for nitrite/ nitrate content after the coral has been left in it for some time. If salt water is used as the cleansing agent, the rocks or coral should be left in a strong solution of this for a week or more, then rinsed and dried.

Substrate: This can be cleaned the same way as the rocks, and the final rinse water should again be tested for nitrite/ nitrate content. You will probably need to do a small quantity at a time in a suitable plastic (never metal) bucket. With regard to the container, this should be of the sort suitable for wine making or food mixing, rather than the cheaper trash can types that are probably made from recycled plastics.

Equipment: It is recommended that all equipment to be placed into the aquarium, and any artificial items, should also be cleaned in a strong saline solution. This ensures that the minimum of airborne bacteria will be on them at the time you undertake the final setting up of your aquarium.

SETTING UP

On the day you decide to set up your marine aquarium you should be sure that you have plenty of time to do this so that it is not left half completed. All of the things you have purchased should be placed close at hand. A final rinsing of everything would not be amiss, after which the following stages can be undertaken.

1. Place the tank in the chosen site, because

once it has water in it you will not be able to lift the weight involved.

2. If an undergravel filter is to be included, this should be the first thing placed into the tank. It should be large enough to cover the entire aquarium floor. The fit must be very snug if maximum performance is expected. Any gap between the filter and the glass walls will allow water to bypass the filter system. To reduce this risk you could apply aquarium sealant to small spaces. If this approach is taken you will have to allow sufficient time for the sealant to harden, so consider this aspect in advance of the setting up day. Fit the up-lift tubes and insert air diffusers and tubing into them if a powerhead or external pump is not the source of water movement.

3. If a powerhead is used, remember that this must fit under the ledge that will support the glass cover plate of the tank. You may need to trim the up-lift tube so that this is possible.

4. The coarse substrate can now be added. This should have a depth of at least 1 1/2in (3.8cm) at the front of the tank. It can then get deeper toward the back, so a nice slope is created. Apart from being visually pleasing it will encourage detritus to fall toward the front glass, where it is more easily removed. It may be wise to erect a retaining wall at some point across the substrate slope. This can be done with either rocks or glass. In the latter case you simply use aquarium bonding seal on two pieces of glass so that an inverted 'T' shape is created. This will minimize the amount of substrate that will drift forward.

5. The coarse substrate can now be covered with a layer of finer sand–but not too much of it. Next, the larger rocks can be

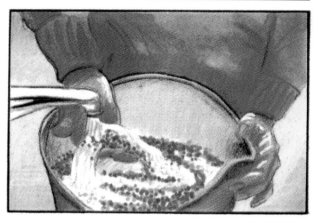

The substrate must be thoroughly rinsed under hot running fresh water.

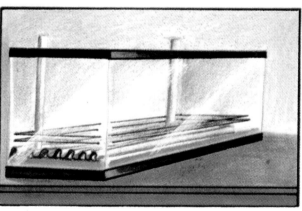

Then the subgravel filter is put into place.

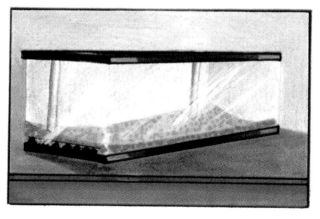

Then the substrate is used to barely cover the undergravel filter.

positioned in the substrate. Remember to leave adequate space at the front of the aquarium for the fish to swim in and so you can see them well.

6. If an external filter system is being used, the inlet head and tubing can be installed just above the substrate at the rear of the tank. This can be held in place by suction pads.

7. The heater/ thermostats can now be placed into position. Be sure that they are clear of the substrate. If two heaters are being used, position them at opposite ends of the tank to obtain good heat circulation. External stick-on thermometers can be positioned at this stage.

8. Coral and smaller rocks, together with artificial plants, can now be placed into the tank and so arranged that they hide as much of the equipment and its tubing as possible. If airstones are included, these can be positioned behind coral or rocks to produce interesting "curtains" of rising bubbles.

All electrical wiring is best fitted into a cable tidy so that it is not trailing all over the place. Be sure to fit non-return valves in the tubing from air pumps. Remember that the cover glass or plastic should have suitable cutouts in it to allow all tubing from the tank to exit to the power filter, pump, or electrical outlets. If glass is used as a cover (rather than plastic), it might be better to have this in two pieces. This will make it easier to feed the fishes, for glass can be heavy and awkward to maneuver.

9. The aquarium hood, with its contained lights, can now be placed onto the tank in order that you can arrange the wiring to your satisfaction. It must then of course be removed so the tank can be filled with water.

The artificial salts can be added directly into the tank at this stage, or later, after the tank is filled. The advantage of adding the salt later is that should the tank leak and have to be emptied, the salt will not have been wasted.

Now fill the tank ... but not with a hose. Fill it with a measured container so you know the actual capacity of the tank.

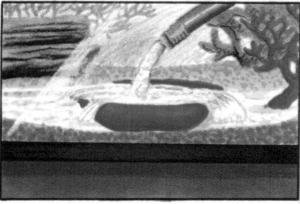

Now you can put in the thermostatically controlled heater, coral and other decorations.

10. The final stage of setting up is to add the water to the tank. With a newly set up aquarium you can mix the salt and water in the aquarium itself (rather than preparing this in buckets as will be done for partial water changes). However, do not use a hose to fill the tank, because by so doing you will not know just how much water the tank, fully furnished, contains. You will need to know this volume in case you have to add medicines at any later date. Normally, the furnishings will displace 10-15% of the potential capacity of the tank, which is never filled to capacity anyway.

Fill the tank from buckets that have been so marked that you can tell exactly how much water is being used. In order that the substrate is not unduly disturbed when the water is poured in, the best way to proceed is as follows. Place a saucer or small plate onto the substrate. Use a jug to take water from the bucket and pour this slowly onto the saucer. Repeat this until you have a reasonable amount of water in the tank. Then you can pour the water into the tank straight from the bucket, but very carefully. When the tank is about half full you can see if there are any last-minute rearrangements to be done. If not, fill the tank to just below the cover glass level, or such that when the hood is fitted you will not see the water line. During this filling stage be very sure none of the electrical appliances are plugged into outlets; this is potentially lethal to you.

Synthetic sea water salts are available from your pet or aquatic dealer. Choose a quality brand recommended by the dealer. This should be added to the tank water and carefully stirred with a

Only use the best of artificial salts. Your aquarium dealer can tell you which is the best according to his/her own experiences.

Try to use all of the salt from the packet (so buy according to likely needs) in order to ensure that all of the trace elements are included in the water mix. Once the initial salt water has been prepared, you can then fit the cover glass and hood onto the tank, then plug everything in. Hopefully, all will be working. If not, unplug all electrical cables before you place your hands in the water to sort out problems.

nonmetallic spoon. Do not attempt to obtain the required specific gravity at this stage, because the water is of course still cold. It is best to underestimate the amount of salt needed as it is easier to add salt than to have to siphon off water that has too high an SG reading.

FINAL CHECKS

If all is well you must now wait until the water has been heated to the desired level. This will be a variable time depending on the tank's capacity, the power of the heaters, and the room temperature. Once this has been reached, you can then check the specific gravity reading.

If it is on the low side you can add more salt. If it is too high you must remove some of the water and replace it with fresh water so that it dilutes the salinity. You can check the ammonia/nitrite levels at this time and make a note of these.

At this point you are no doubt very anxious to obtain some fishes-but this urge must be resisted. It will take a few weeks, even a month or so, for the water to mature. The colonization of the filters with nitrifying bacteria is dependent on the amount of nitrogenous compounds that are present in the aquarium. You can help matters in one of three ways.

1. You could purchase special cultures that contain the beneficial bacteria wanted from your dealer.

2. You could ask a friend with a well established (and healthy) marine aquarium if he or she would give you some of the substrate material from their tank. This will be rich in beneficial bacteria.

3. You could place any nitrogenous compound in the tank in very small amounts. This will decay and provide a ready source of food for the required bacteria, which will then start to build up the size of their colonies. Such items as fish food, slivers of meat or fish, in fact anything of a protein origin, will suffice.

Once a week you can check the SG of the water and the nitrite/nitrate levels. Initially, the nitrite levels will be high. They will steadily fall as the nitrifying bacteria get to work, and as algae begin to become established on the rocks, coral, and glass panels. Only when the nitrite level is below 0.1mg/ liter should you think in terms of adding fishes–and then only one or two that are of a hardy type. The ecosystem must be developed on a very gradual basis. Attempts to rush matters will only result in disaster, and all of your careful preparations will have been for nothing: you will have to start all over again. The key to success in any form of fishkeeping lies in the preparation of the watery world in which the fishes live. The better this is, the less chance there will be of "new tank syndrome" and the loss of initial stock.

ROUTINE MAINTENANCE

1. Water Temperature: Make it a habit to check this every time you view the aquarium. Always have a replacement heater available; it will cost you a lot less than most of your fishes.

2. Fishes: Check daily to see that they are all present. Any that are missing should be located. If they are dead, they must be removed. if they are just missing, could they have jumped out of the aquarium? If not, perhaps one of the other fishes ate them.

3. Specific Gravity: Check this weekly and never allow it to move too far from your favored level.

4. pH: Check this weekly and adjust as needed. It should never fall below a reading of 8.

5. Excess Algae: Should this be a problem on the front viewing panel, it can be removed using a nonmetal scraper obtained from your pet store. You can feed the algae to the fishes.

6. Water Changes: These can be made weekly (about 10%) or once a month (about 20-30%) depending on how well the aquarium

is functioning. Such changes should take account of water lost through evaporation.

7. Substrate Cleaning: Weekly. You can use a siphon or a gravel cleaner obtained from your pet store. Rake the substrate very carefully about once a month in order to remove any accumulated debris.

8. Cover Glass: Clean weekly. Dust on this will greatly reduce the amount of light that enters the aquarium.

9. Air and Pump Lines: Check all connections periodically to ensure they are still watertight or not loose.

10. Filters: You will get to know how quickly these need cleaning. Never leave them to chance, so regular inspection is the recommended course.

11. Nitrates or Nitrites: Check *at least* every two weeks—weekly if the aquarium is small.

12. Oxygen: Remember, if you add invertebrates to your aquarium these consume oxygen; is there enough for both them and the fish?

13. Lighting: Bulbs will need replacing about every 9 months even though they are still functioning. Clean tubes regularly so that they do not lose efficiency because of dust. Unplug them while you are cleaning them.

14. Back-up Power: An established marine aquarium is a valuable property. You should consider what would happen in a prolonged power failure. Look into the possibility of using battery power to provide emergency aeration and filtration.

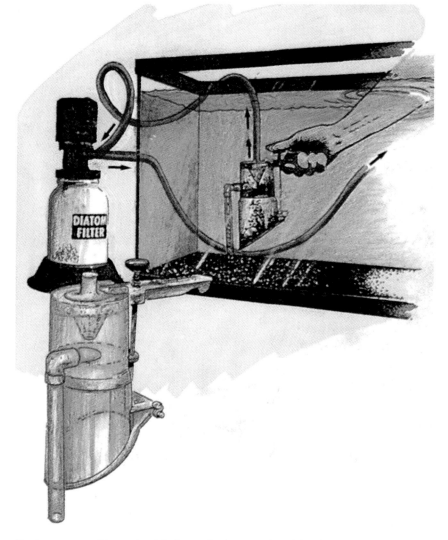

Back-up power filters should always be kept on hand for the emergency situation ... like someone dropping cigarette ashes into the tank. Here an accessory to the Vortex diatom filter is the gravel-cleaning attachment being used as shown.

Selection & Preparation

In the chapter "Environment " you read about "Expected Losses." It is recommended that you reread that section again to refresh your memory before going out and purchasing marine fishes. Here we can discuss the whole question of fish acquisition in more detail, because it is such a vital part of getting off to a good start. You should already be aware that most marine species are taken from their natural habitat and that this can create problems. What you cannot always be sure about are the methods used to capture the fishes. This has a considerable bearing on their likely longevity.

Basically, there are two ways in which fishes can be caught, by netting or by stunning. Only the first named is desirable.

The best method is when local inhabitants supplement their income by catching just a few fishes at a time in small nets. This is quite a common part of day to day life on the islands of Indonesia, such as Bali, in the Pacific ocean. The fishes are handled very carefully because the fishermen never catch too many at a time and can ill afford losses. Fishes can also be caught using much larger nets–still a safe method but with rather more losses to be expected.

The least desirable methods of capture involve the use of cyanide or other drugs, or by using explosives. In both of these methods the object is to stun many fish and simply gather them as they float on the surface. Clearly, a

Dr. Cliff Emmens, a leading authority on marine aquariums, maintains this tank in his home. It features lots of living marine plants.

large number of fishes die in the process. Even many of those that survive may have been badly shocked and may never fully recover. Many other species of marine life are killed in the process. The method allows for the fishes to be gathered in large numbers and sold at a lower cost than those gathered using nets and other humane traps.

When you go into your local pet or aquatic store there usually is no way you can know how the fishes have been caught; even the dealer may not know. It therefore comes down to a situation of trust built up over years, both by the consumer (you) and by the dealers with those who supply their stores. As dealers must carefully select their suppliers based on performance, so you must do likewise. If you see marine fishes advertised at prices much lower than most dealers seem to be selling them at, you should be suspicious. As with most things in life, you will generally get what you pay for.

WHERE TO PURCHASE FISHES

Without a doubt your best source is your local pet or aquatic dealer. A good store will have an experienced staff who can give you in-depth information about marine fishkeeping and will they carry the variety of equipment you will want as you progress.

There may be no importers in your area, and dealing with mail order companies carries many risks. You cannot be sure just how good they are unless you have visited their establishment at some time or they are highly recommended to you by a friend who has dealt with them for a period of time. With your local pet dealers you can see their tanks, see the fishes before you purchase, and can drop in anytime to discuss problems you may encounter. Nor do you necessarily pay more for these advantages. I have seen fishes from other sources at higher prices than in reputable local aquatic stores.

Visit as many stores as you can so that you can compare standards and prices. In the long run, the prices charged are not so important as the standard of after-sales service you receive. Support the store that is very clean, has a good display of tanks, a fine range of equipment, and friendly staff who you feel confident are trying to advise you, rather than just sell you as much as they can.

Remember, if you purchase your tank, equipment, and

especially the fishes, from a number of sources, you are not as likely to develop as good a relationship with your dealer as when you obtain most of your needs from a single source. An important initial consideration with regard to the fishes is that if you purchase them from numerous sources it would be impossible to pinpoint which fish from which source was the problem in the event that things went wrong. This being so, it is recommended that you obtain your first fishes from the same dealer. An additional benefit of this is that you can match the SG and the temperature of your quarantine tank to that of the dealer's tanks. By taking such a course you will reduce the chances of stress created by the sudden changes in water properties.

Even a healthy-looking fish like this *Centropyge heraldi* can harbor disease organisms that have not yet caused the fish to decline, but one way to avoid disease is to purchase from a reputable and knowledgeable dealer who recognizes and segregates sick stock.

HEALTH

You will obviously want your fishes to be in good health, so inspect each purchase with great care. Their colors should be bold and not faded, this applying to any body markings they may exhibit. The fins should be entire, with no signs of rotting, damage, or abrasions. The fishes should swim easily, and in an upright manner. Those that are seen to suddenly dash across their tank or rub against rocks are probably harboring parasites that they are trying to rid themselves of. Fishes that swim on an angle might have an internal problem with their swim bladder, the organ that enables them to ascend and descend in the water, as well as to keep

Opposite: The aquarium world rose in protest when it was discovered that Filipino fish collectors used cyanide to stun the fish before they captured them. This killed reefs and eventually the fishes died from poisoning. This shows a Filipino collecting reef fishes.

them in an upright position. Alternatively, they may be badly stressed, have a digestive problem, or suffer from a congenital disorder.

The eyes of fishes should be round and clear; any that exhibit cotton-like growths or an opaqueness have a problem. The scales should lie smooth, never standing out from the skin. There should be no fungal growth, abrasions, or obvious signs of a problem, such as parasitic wounds, on the fishes. The body should be full, never emaciated or bloated. If a fish is seen hanging near the surface or within the streams of bubbles from an airstone, it is usually because it has a respiratory problem. Its gills may be seen to open and close very rapidly as

It takes experience to recognize abnormal fish behavior, but a few hints are given in the illustration below.

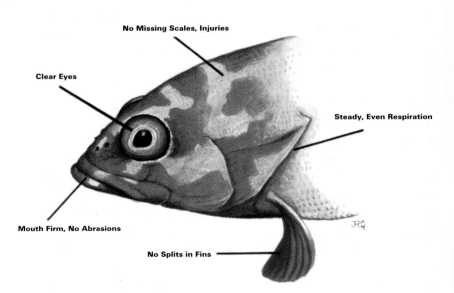

No Missing Scales, Injuries

Clear Eyes

Steady, Even Respiration

Mouth Firm, No Abrasions

No Splits in Fins

it tries to obtain sufficient oxygen.

A point of note with regard to the fin positions of marine fishes is that if they are lying close to the body this does not necessarily mean they are ill. In freshwater species this is a sign that things are not well. Many marine fishes swim with fins close to their body.

THE DEALER

Much emphasis has been placed on the value of a good dealer, so what can you expect of such a person? He or she should be willing to let you see the fishes eating, should be happy to show you the quarantine tanks on the premises, and will tell you just how long the fishes have been in the store. If you are just purchasing your tank and its furnishings they will (should!) not try to sell you fishes at this time, but will advise you on setting up

procedures. If they try to sell you an extra tank for quarantine purposes, this is not hard sell but sound advice which you should take.

Try to visit a store a number of times before you commit yourself to the purchase of the fishes. You can observe how the assistants handle fishes being sold. Harsh netting of fishes is not a good sign; this should always be gentle. Even better is when the fishes are seen to be caught with jars or by being ushered with nets into plastic bags.

THE VALUE OF QUARANTINE

The object of quarantining, or isolating, all fishes purchased is to ensure that they are as healthy as possible before they are placed into an established ecosystem. In a newly set up aquarium this can be, and often is, the quarantine tank for the first purchases. However, this is by no means an ideal situation. Some of the pathogenic organisms may well be able to survive in the aquarium a long time after they have killed the fishes. This being so, you are strongly advised to have a separate quarantine tank.

SPECIES SELECTION

One of the basic ground rules for keeping any livestock in a confined area is that they must be compatible with any other animals that they share the accommodations with. If this prerequisite is not met you are simply asking for trouble. Some fishes will bully, attack, or even eat others kept in the same aquarium. Even if they cannot physically injure other species they may stress them by their very presence. This can apply to fishes of the same sort, because although a given species may live happily with their own kind in the enormous expanse of an ocean, things can be totally different when there is insufficient room for each individual to control its own territory in an aquarium.

You must therefore select the initial fishes for your aquarium with great care. Discuss them with your dealer and take his or her advice. Compatibility of a number of popular marine species is indicated in the chapter on marine species. You also want hardy species that are known to be able to withstand the less-than ideal conditions the novice is likely to have in relation to water conditions. Do not be tempted to begin with a given species because it is especially colorful or beautiful. Fishes such as anemonefishes and damselfishes are popular and colorful enough for the novice, yet are a little more forgiving of water conditions than many other species. This does not mean they are hardy by freshwater standards, however.

During the period in which your aquarium water is "maturing," read as much about the species you are interested in as possible. Talk to dealers about the virtues and problems of such species. Avoid at all costs having fishes of differing sizes in the aquarium, as this invariably leads to problems. Carnivorous fishes that will not bother individuals of their own or similar size will have no compulsions about gobbling up that new little gem you have just added to the community tank.

TRANSPORTING FISH

Once your quarantine tank is up and running you can then make your

Epinephelus lanceolatus and many other fishes in the family Serranidae will swallow just about any tankmate they can fit into their mouths.

Chaetodon species have modified mouth parts to enable them to pick small bits of food out of the many tiny crevices found in every coral reef.

initial fish purchase. Restrict this to one or two fish only. This may not be what you originally had in mind, but hopefully the text this far has persuaded you on the merits of progressing in small steps, based on success, rather than attempting too much too soon and ending up totally disillusioned.

When you collect your fishes, tell the dealer how far away you live, as this will have an influence on how the fishes are packed. If your journey home is likely to be lengthy, the dealer may use oxygen, rather than just air, in the plastic bag. Alternatively, a much larger bag will be provided that contains more air. The bag should then be placed into a larger and darkened bag so that the fishes will not be stressed by the daylight when you leave the store. Better still on long

journeys would be to place the bag into a polystyrene or cardboard box. This will provide greater heat insulation, and I am sure you would feel happier carrying this. Do not stop to do other shopping once you have the fishes, but get home as quickly, yet safely, as possible.

STOCKING THE AQUARIUM

Once at home the plastic bag containing the fishes should be floated on the surface of the quarantine tank's water. The tank should not be lit at this stage or it will startle and stress the fishes that have been housed in total darkness for some length of time. The purpose of floating the bag on the surface is so that the two bodies of water will begin to equate with each other. After about 15 minutes or so you can open the plastic bag and allow some of its water to escape, being replaced with that from the isolation tank. This procedure can be repeated about three or four times over the next 20 to 30 minutes. By this time the two bodies of water will be similar.

The fishes will have had some time to adjust to any differences in the SG and pH values, assuming these were relatively small in the first place. Now you can open the neck of the bag a final time and allow the fishes to swim gently out. The isolation tank is to be their home for the next 14-21 days. At the end of this period you will repeat the procedure of transferring them to their final home, the display aquarium. During the isolation period it is important to try and maintain the water conditions of the isolation tank so that they are the same as in the main display tank. This will make it much

easier for the fishes to adjust one more time when they are transferred.

If you do not have an isolation tank then of course you will have to transfer the fishes directly into your prepared display tank. Be very sure, however, that in this instance the aquarium water has matured, that the biological filter is working, and that you are obtaining zero or near zero nitrite readings. If all goes well you can then add more fishes, one (at the most two) at a time until you have reached the maximum stocking capacity.

As you add more fishes to an established aquarium it is important that you closely study the reactions of the other fishes. The newcomer

Opposite: The new fish must be acclimated to the water temperature before being put into the tank. This is easily done by floating the plastic bag in the aquarium.

may be a troublemaker. It may be very timid, and thus be harassed by the other tankmates. Your aquarium is just like your immediate neighborhood. Every new neighbor is an unknown entity until he, she, or they have settled in. Some are a joy to have–others you may wish had never come. With your aquarium you have one major advantage. If the latest acquisition does not fit in you can remove it or remove other inhabitants of the miniature world you are creating. When watching new arrivals settle in, bear in mind that the best time to really see how things are developing is when the main tank lights are switched off. This is when each fish retreats to its own little resting area, and when disagreements can start with newcomers until the latter has found its own place in its new home.

Before buying an expensive fish, observe it for a while in your dealer's tank. Try to watch it feed. A ravenous fish is usually a healthy one.

Pet shops usually carry an extensive line of fish foods. Buy several different brands and alternate them. Regardless of the claims, no one has perfected a completely balanced diet for marine fishes.

Feeding Marine Fishes

The most singular feeding problem that the marine aquarist has, when compared to those keeping freshwater species, is that the freshwater fishes will probably have been reared in captivity and so are quite familiar with commercially prepared foods. Wild-caught marine fishes must be conditioned to accepting foods they may never have seen before. It is for this reason that you should see the fishes eating before purchasing them. Indeed, stay near the tank in the dealer's store after the fishes have eaten so that you can see whether or not they regurgitate the food a minute or so later, as can sometimes happen.

Feeding serves a number of functions. It is a means of supplying the body with a fuel to generate energy needed in movement and other activities. It provides the basic ingredients the fishes require to build bodily tissue and to develop immune systems against diseases. It is also of social importance, both in enabling fish of the same species to learn to live together and in relaxing them. Feeding and fear are antagonistic, so a stressed or nervous fish will not eat, or will eat very little. This is why a fish that is eating well indicates to you that conditions are at least satisfactory and the fish is not feeling stressed.

Feeding is also an acquired habit to a certain degree. Young fishes eat what they see older fishes eat; they generally ignore what they do not see others eat. By the time a fish is

Holacanthus tricolor

mature its diet is well established and it will not readily take that which it is unfamiliar with. Even predatory species will have developed preferences for certain prey species, either because the latter are convenient or because the individual fish has developed a particular talent for catching a given prey, and so tends to seek out that prey in preference to others, even if the latter are more readily available.

All of these factors should be considered when trying to supply a well rounded diet to a tank community. Always remember, however, that a community of fishes is a collection of individuals, and it is the individual you are feeding, not the community. If this point is not foremost in your mind, you will tend to assume that because a given food is known to be taken by a given species it will be taken by any member of that species. This will result in your not devoting time to watching your fishes eat, but simply putting a given amount of food in the aquarium.

Fishes have their preferences for certain foods. Apart from this fact, you can learn a great deal more by watching them eat. You will soon become aware of the timid ones, the greedy eaters, and those that ignore certain kinds of food. For those in the last category you must endeavor to find an alternative item that they will more readily accept. For all fishes, their behavior is the first indication you will have if they are not well. Feeding provides you with a situation of normalcy by which all

Seahorses like this *Hippocampus kuda* are among the troublesome species when it comes to feeding, which is why they often are set up in aquariums housing them alone.

Balistes vetula

other behaviors can be judged. If a fish shows no interest in coming for its food, or toys with it, you can suspect a problem and either remove the fish for a more isolated observation, or simply keep a very watchful eye on it over the next 48 hours.

FEEDING HABITS

All fish species have developed feeding habits based on two criteria. One is with respect to the kinds of food they eat, the other is in relation to the environment in which the food is eaten. Taking the kinds of food eaten first, species can be categorized into one of three types:

1. **Carnivores.** (predators). These species live predominantly on the flesh of other organisms. These may be other fishes,

invertebrates, or both. It should be mentioned that the term carnivore does not necessarily mean that the fish will attack all other fishes in an aquarium as is sometimes thought by the beginner.

Lantern Bass, *Serranus baldwini*

Some species, such as seahorses and pipefishes, eat very small invertebrates and are no danger to other peaceful fishes in the aquarium. This is in comparison to the real predators, like lionfishes, which will attack anything smaller than themselves, or that will fit into their mouths. However, a fish does not need to be a carnivore to be a danger in an aquarium. Some fishes are naturally aggressive and will nip the fins of other species. Still others will not tolerate their own kind in close proximity. They will fight to the point that wounds are inflicted, which are an obvious source of secondary invasion by parasites or other pathogens.

2. Omnivores. These species eat a certain amount of live foods, but they also graze on small algae, as well as the larger seaweeds. Some omnivores are more carnivorous than others, while some could almost be regarded as being herbivorous.

3. **Herbivores.** These species are the plant eaters, but even these eat microscopic life forms that are on the plants eaten. It should

be mentioned that the food habits of these fishes must be taken into consideration when decorating your aquarium if you want to include plant life.

Barred Hamlet, *Hypoplectrus puella*

With regard to the environment in which the fishes eat, species can be broadly divided into three types:

1. Those that feed in open waters, either near the surface or at mid depths.

Indigo Hamlet, *Hypoplectrus indigo*

2. Those that feed on or near the substrate.

3. Those that browse on reefs and rocks.

Additionally, some fishes are nocturnal, others diurnal (daytime), and still others crepuscular (dawn and dusk) feeders. Given

Harlequin Bass, *Serranus tigrinus*

these various types, it will be appreciated that to expect a given species to settle down and feed in an aquarium that does not provide the sort of conditions it prefers will only make things

Chalk Bass, *Serranus tortugarum*

more difficult for the hobbyist. The fishes will feel insecure, thus stressed, therefore less willing to eat readily. When selecting species, give careful consideration to the known feeding types and habitats preferred by the fishes. Further, try to make your selection such that you have a mixture of types (but avoid very predatory fishes in a community tank). This will ensure that each species occupies a certain area of the aquarium; the fishes will not all be competing for food and territories in the same places.

Until experience is gained keep only fishes of reasonably comparable sizes.

A VARIED DIET

Marine fish feeding is still very much in its infancy. The only sure way you can supply all the needs of the fishes is to provide a very varied selection of foods. By so doing you greatly reduce the possibility that some important vitamin, mineral, or essential ingredient is missing. Make notes on what foods are preferred by the species you keep— and never be afraid to experiment (a little at a time) with new foods. Initially, you should continue feeding your fishes the exact diet given to you by the dealer. Once the fishes have settled into their new home you can then broaden the diet if you feel it could be improved.

Butter Hamlet, *Hypoplectrus unicolor*

HOW OFTEN TO FEED?

The number of feedings your fishes will receive during the day is clearly linked to your own work routine. By preference, most species will prefer to have small feedings, but several of them. When you first introduce the fishes to your aquarium they will be rather nervous, so they will not eat a great deal. This

Shy Hamlet, *Hypoplectrus guttavarius*

Tobacco Bass, *Serranus tabacarius*

being so, too much food will be wasted and therefore be a possible source of pollution. Feed two small meals a day during the first week, then increase the number and quantity of meals based on the appetites of the fishes. As a general guide, the fishes should only be fed what they will consume in about 2-3 minutes.

Spotted Moray, *Gymnothorax moringa*

each day and, where families are concerned, establish strict routines as to who is to be feeding the fishes. You do not want everyone putting in food because they thought the fishes hadn't been fed by another family member.

Bear in mind that fishes utilize their food rather better than we do, so you should never risk overfeeding. Omnivorous species are probably the easiest to feed because they will find quite a lot to eat in the aquarium, so are unlikely to ever be starving. Try to feed the fishes at the same time

COMMERCIAL FISH FOODS

The quality and variety of foods you can now purchase for fishes is extensive. Most such foods are those developed for freshwater species, with maybe a few additives to make them more palatable for marine species when the label states "for marine fishes." All foods, whether for fishes, dogs, cats, or birds, contain much the same ingredients. It is the ratio of one ingredient to the other that determines its value and of course the form in which it is presented.

The three common ingredients to nearly all foods are proteins, fats, and carbohydrates. Proteins are rich in amino acids. They are used for building tissue and repairing that which is damaged or worn out through muscular activity. Fats are prime sources of energy, as well as providing insulation tissue and aiding the transportation of other compounds in the blood stream. Carbohydrates are essentially energy foods,

Longfin Darnselfish, *Stegastes diencaeus*

Bicolor Darnselfish, *Stegastes partitus*

Night Sergeant, *Abudefduf taurus*

though they also provide bulk to a diet and serve numerous other functions as well. The undoubted advantage of quality commercial foods is that they are carefully prepared to provide each of these vital ingredients.

Sunshine Damselfish, *Chromis insolatus*

Furthermore, commercial foods are also fortified with all of the vitamins and minerals needed by your fishes, which are often destroyed or changed in composition during the food preparation processes. Commercial foods are sold in many forms, each prepared in order to cater to the wide-ranging requirements of fishes and to provide the sort of alternatives that might encourage a fish to sample them. The differing forms of the foods available to you are as follows:

1. **Flakes.** These can be fast or slow sinking. They are very concentrated and absorb water once immersed into it. As a result, care must be taken that too many are not placed into the water. What seems very little to you can represent a feast to the fishes. There are many types of flake foods, some prepared as staple diets, others as tonic foods. Some are essentially vegetable and carbohydrate in content; others have a higher protein content, so be sure to read the label and any literature (if this is available) with them so that you can obtain the correct flakes for your needs.

2. **Tablets.**

These, too, can be fast or slow sinking. You can also stick some of them onto the glass panels so that the fishes can nibble at them as required. For small fish species you can break the tablets up as you can with flake foods. You could totally crush them and make a solution with them by adding aquarium water. In this form they will appeal to filter feeders such as corals, though it is recommended that beginners not keep live corals until experience has been gained with water properties.

3. **Liquids.**

There are a number of liquid foods available

Longfin Damselfish, *Stegastes diencaeus*

Yellow Damselfish, *Stegastes planifrons*

Yellowtail Damselfish, *Microspathodon chrysurus*

that will be useful for invertebrates and fish fry, but again these will not normally be needed by the first time marine fishkeeper.

4. **Sticks.** These will float for quite a while on the surface of the water. They will appeal to the open water species that are adapted to taking food from the surface.

5. **Freeze Dried.** Just about any live food can be killed and freeze dried. These are concentrated forms of food that may include such items as meats, shrimp, lobsters, crab meat, various worms, and numerous eggs of both fishes and crustaceans. They are very safe forms of food because they are free of pathogens.

6. **Frozen.** Commercial frozen fish foods, like freeze dried foods, have the advantage that they are very safe. Again, just about all natural fish foods, such as shrimp and other crustaceans,

and fishes themselves, can be frozen. They are easily kept in the freezer compartment of a refrigerator and can be thawed out as needed.

7. **Live Foods.** A number of live food cultures are produced commercially and sold in pet shops. These include brine shrimp, *Artemia salina*, an excellent natural food that is very popular with freshwater enthusiasts as a food for young fishes. *Daphnia*, a tiny freshwater crustacean, is another live food that marine fishes will enjoy. Tubifex worms are popular with some enthusiasts, but not with all, because they live in sewage, mud banks, and similar places. Unless cleansed in fresh water they carry with them the risk of introducing parasites. It is not necessary here to describe the culture methods because instructions come with the foods. Always remember that live

Frozen foods are among the favorites for marine fishes. They keep fresh and can even be fed in the frozen form without being thawed out. Pet shops normally carry many different kinds of fresh-frozen fish foods.

freshwater foods will not live long in the marine aquarium, so feed sparingly so that they do not die and create pollution. Feed worms in floating feeders available at your pet or aquatic store.

NON-COMMERCIAL FOODS

Given the wide range of commercial foods it is not really necessary to feed any others to your fishes, but most hobbyists will experiment in order to broaden the menu. The first rule when feeding noncommercial foods is to be very sure it is clean. You can chop up any of the numerous marine species sold in stores: lobsters, crabs, squid, shrimp, and even fishes. Of course, such foods may contain potentially harmful organisms unless it is well boiled first. You can suspend bits of fish and other meats on some string for your fishes to nibble on, but remove it once it starts to decay.

Vegetable matter for marine species is usually in the form of algae grown in the aquarium. However, if you have more herbivores than algae to feed them, you can provide extra fresh vegetable matter in one of two ways. You could set up an algae tank by placing some clean rocks into this and leaving it in a sunny position. You do not need to filter or aerate the water, though the latter will provide for a more vigorous colony of algae. If required, you could brightly illuminate the tank. The algae can be scraped off the rocks, or they can simply be placed into the marine tank periodically as needed.

The second option is to provide a variety of vegetables from your kitchen, duly chopped into small pieces. Spinach, lettuce, kale, indeed any green foods, as well as carrots, can be offered. You can also purchase seaweed powders from your pet shop. You could also float or submerge larger pieces of vegetation in the aquarium, but remove them once they are clearly decaying. The same is true of freshwater aquatic plants that can also be used for feeding your fishes.

Non-vegetable foods include boiled egg yolk, finely chopped cheese, and shredded beef. These foods may not be natural to marine fishes but are used consistently by freshwater fishkeepers. Commercial fish foods are also not natural foods to marine fishes, so do not be afraid of a little experimentation. The important thing is that you supply a wide enough variety of foods that you can persuade the fishes to eat at least some of them.

Check with your dealer for
the frozen foods he
recommends for your
marine fishes.

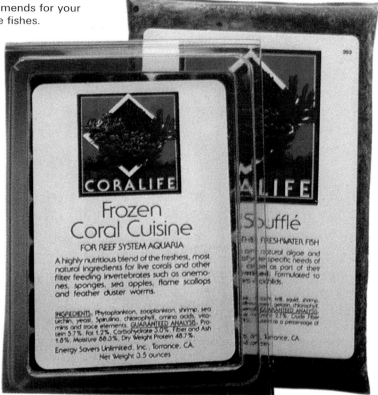

Where predatory
fishes are being kept
you may need to supply
them with live fishes,
at least until they are
settled in and you can
try to persuade them to
take commercial foods.
The most popular live
fish species used as
food will be small
goldfish, because they
are inexpensive and
widely available.
Guppies and mollies
are two other species,
and ones that will
survive a little longer in
the saline waters of the
marine aquarium. The
idea of feeding live
fishes to your marine

species may not appeal to you at all. The answer is therefore to select omnivorous or herbivorous species that will not require live fishes.

an ample supply of algae growing in the aquarium. It is best to prepare little sachets of food to leave for friends to give to the fishes each day or every other

Sunshine Damselfish, *Chromis insolatus*, at a differnet growth stage from the same species shown on page 166.

VACATION FEEDING

It is very important that when you go on vacation the fishes are not overfed by well intentioned but uninformed friends or relatives. Marine fishes cannot be left for such long periods without food as can freshwater species, unless they are herbivores and there is

day. Impress on them the dangers of overfeeding and that the food you have prepared is ample for the fishes because they also feed on organisms and algae in the tank. Some aquatic and pet stores offer a "fish-sitting" service which may be worth the cost involved if you have expensive marines.

The feeding of marine fishes is not in itself a problem. The problem is in convincing the fishes that the alternatives you are providing to them that are so different from their natural diet are acceptable foods. Keep the tank substrate and rocks clear of uneaten food, and try to make sure that the fishes you purchase are already taking commercial foods. Once your fishes are eating well, any additional fishes will be encouraged to sample what they see others eating, so it is the early days that are invariably the most difficult.

Freeze dried foods are a very nourishing and safe food for marine fishes.

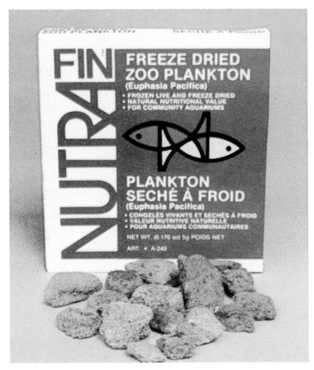

Keeping Fishes Healthy

If the pet goldfish owner represents the most casual extreme of fishkeeping, the marine hobbyist is the total opposite–or must be if his fishes are to survive. If you take the view that your fishes always have a problem that is simply waiting to develop, you will commence with the correct attitude toward fish health. All fishes and all bodies of water house within them countless pathogens of one sort or another. These will range from macroorganisms to microorganisms–those you can see and those that require high-powered microscopes to be viewed.

A fish can only develop immunity to given pathogens by being exposed to them in very small doses over an extended period of time. Its body is attacked by the pathogens on a small scale, and special body cells attack the pathogenic bacteria. If they kill the bacteria the fish lives, but if they fail to do so the fish becomes more ill and eventually dies or, in the wild state, will be eaten by a predator. The fishes that survive now have an internal "catalog" of these pathogens. When another attack comes the immune system can quickly recognize the bacteria concerned. The bacteria are engulfed and destroyed, and the fish thus appears again to be fit and healthy.

In the vast expanse of an ocean the pathogens are kept in check by the simple process of dilution. Currents sweep them away, while the fishes themselves also move over considerable distances compared to the situation in what is a very tiny volume of water in even the largest of aquariums. In their native habitat the fishes live in very stable conditions and in an ecosystem that has developed over millions of years. This is in total contrast to the situation in your aquarium. In the aquarium you have probably introduced rocks, corals, and other furnishings that are totally unknown to the fishes you keep. More important, the bacteria in the air and water of your homeland will be different from that of the oceanic habitat of your fishes. This means that their immune system will not recognize the pathogens, so it will take time for it to be fully operative, always assuming it is only exposed to low levels of invasion.

The fact that the fishes will have been transferred through a number of differing conditions from the time they are taken from the

The oceanic environment from which most marine aquarium species come is characterized by great stability, and abrupt changes in water composition and other factors can be very harmful.

sea or ocean to the time they arrive in your aquarium merely compounds matters. They must contend with a great deal in a relatively short space of time, such as:

1. Differing SG values.
2. Differing pH values.
3. Sudden temperature changes.
4. Fluctuations in oxygen availability.
5. Unfamiliar foods and the lack of food (during transportation).
6. Being netted and handled.
7. Differing light intensities.
8. Differing environmental conditions (rocks, plants, etc.).
9. Differing coinhabitants of their accommodation at a given moment in time.
10. Differing bacteria, fungi, and parasites in their environment.
11. The shock of seeing giants (people) and other animals staring at them.

This is akin to your suddenly being dragged from your home and the people you know and being taken from one place to another by creatures you have never seen, to eventually be placed in a tropical swampland where conditions and the food are totally alien to you. Of one thing you can be sure—you will be ill to a greater or lesser degree. If you think about this situation every time you acquire an additional marine fish, you will never become blase and treat fishes as objects rather than delicate life forms. As it happens, the cost of marine fishes may help you in this direction.

THE SPREAD OF DISEASE

Diseases of fishes are bacterial, viral, or fungal in origin. A virus is really only a living crystal, while fungi are of course of plant origin. They are spread among fishes in a community in a number of ways. Some are carried in the air until they reach water, others are found on any food item, and still others rely on carriers, be they insects, birds, mammals, the fishes themselves, or you the hobbyist. Some complete their life cycle on the host, while others need an intermediate carrier in order to go through the different stages of their life cycle. Such carriers may not themselves be affected by the pathogen.

Many pathogenic bacteria die within a short space of time if they cannot alight on a new host once the one they are on dies. Others can form cysts that can survive long periods of time, this being true of most fungi. They can also withstand extremes of temperature, often well beyond the range the fishes can tolerate. However, they will die once a given level of heat or cold is reached. Given these various

How aggressive or predacious a fish may be has nothing to do with how rugged it may be under aquarium conditions; moray eels like this *Gymnothorax* species can be much less hardy than peaceful cardinalfishes.

facts you will appreciate that you can never eradicate the diseases, only keep them in check. To remove pathogens completely you would have to provide sterile conditions for the fishes, and fishes cannot live in such conditions.

Actually, healthy fishes are able to withstand the onslaught of diseases quite well.

THE PREVENTIVE APPROACH

The worn-out cliche of "prevention is better than cure" still holds good to this day, and it is very much applicable to marine fishes. The vast majority of problems encountered by fishkeepers, of any sort, are invariably attributable to mismanagement on behalf of the aquarist. However, even with the best of management problems will still occur. It is thus a case of doing the best you can and then reacting in a sensible manner once a fish has contracted ill health.

Poor water conditions are the major source of most illnesses because they are the ideal conditions under which pathogens can multiply, thus overwhelming the natural defenses of the fishes. Stress and fear are the next biggest killers of marine fishes. Fear is relatively easily identified because a fish will panic and seek refuge from an obvious aggressor. Stress is very much more difficult to pinpoint because it is a more subtle psychological condition. A fish is not fearful if the SG of the water is incorrect, but its brain is affected. This in turn affects metabolic performance, because defense systems are triggered into action and these slow down, or shut off, other systems-such as the digestive system. The presence of unfamiliar fishes will

Halichoeres garnoti. Fishes with delicate colors lose their color when they become ill. You must therefore watch them for color or behavioral changes.

create stress even though there is no direct threat. The fish may not really be afraid of the other fishes, but something tells its brain that all is not as it should be.

Stressed and fearful fish use up much more energy than do relaxed individuals, yet their food intake drops below the needed level. This means that if pathogens are in the water in numbers they can quickly overwhelm the fish's immune system, so the condition goes from bad to worse.

By being diligent with respect to water conditions, and trying to design the aquarium ecosystem with great care and consideration for the species that it will house, you will already be doing a great deal to minimize the risk of disease rearing its ugly head. But this is only possible once the fishes are acquired, so you must first ensure they are in good health before they are even placed into the furnished aquarium.

THE QUARANTINE TANK

The question of quarantining fishes–and many other animals that are regarded as being delicate–is not without its negative features. However, on balance the benefits far outweigh the potential pitfalls. Let us first consider the pitfalls.

1. Quarantine only has merit if the conditions in the isolation tank are as near to ideal as you can get them. If they are not, the fish may actually contract a problem while in the tank.

2. Because the quarantine tank, of necessity, is sparsely furnished, this could actually stress a fish that had been kept in a well furnished aquarium. This is thus not conducive to the objective of the isolation period.

3. The very fact that a fish is to spend a relatively short period of time in the quarantine tank (14-21 days) means that it will be subjected to one more movement (being transferred to the display tank) than some might consider advantageous.

4. Not all diseases may show themselves within the quarantine period, and this would support the view that it is therefore just another trauma for the fish to go through.

On the benefit side of the equation are the following advantages.

1. If a fish has a disease when you obtain it, even though it shows no visible signs of this, it is better to treat it in isolation. If it dies, it is better doing this away from other tank inhabitants to whom the pathogens would otherwise quickly migrate.

2. You are better able to observe a single fish,

Abudefduf saxatilis. Fishes with clamped fins and gaping mouths are almost surely ill.

or a few fishes, under conditions that enable you to see the fish at all times. In the furnished aquarium, a fish will naturally seek out dark and secluded spots when it feels ill. You may not notice it until the condition has progressed beyond redemption.

3. Treatments for diseases are not always selective in the bacteria they kill. They will destroy the beneficial bacteria of the biological filter as well as the nonpathogenic bacteria that live within the body of all fishes and which are essential to the synthesis of certain vitamins. To thus treat the water of a well established aquarium in order to treat one or two fish is not sound husbandry. It could create problems that did not exist until the treatment was put into play.

4. Apart from screening for parasites or disease, the quarantine tank enables

you to devote special attention to the feeding of newly acquired fishes. You can be certain they receive the food placed into the tank. This is especially important for the more timid or shy feeders, and gets them off to a good start.

THE QUARANTINE OR HOSPITAL TANK

The quarantine tank need only be relatively small when compared to your display aquarium, depending on how large that is. It is therefore not a costly unit to have. It does not need a biological filter, because any medicines used would probably kill the nitrifying bacteria. A simple sponge filter in the tank is adequate, or you could utilize an external power filter for a large quarantine tank. This should not contain charcoal if medicines are used. This is because the carbon will adsorb the medicine and thus render it of almost no value.

It should have an air supply, via a diffuser, if no external power filter is being used. The air will ensure good oxygen content and create water circulation. The heater is best placed in a simple plastic guard so there will be no risk of the fishes being burned should they choose to swim close to it. This is much more likely with ill fishes, which often seek the warmest places in the aquarium. There is no need for a substrate, as this would merely increase the risk of pollution. Some hobbyists place a layer of colored marbles on the base, but these are not essential. You could stand the tank on a sand or similar colored surface, rather than on one that is white.

You will need two thermometers, and of course a glass or plastic cover. Lighting will be needed and, finally, you could place one or two ceramic or weighted (but not with metal) plastic flower pots, or a well cleaned rock, into the tank so the fish has something there to help give it a sense of

once the fish is transferred from one to the other. This poses a dilemma. Are you to maintain the quarantine tank continuously, or

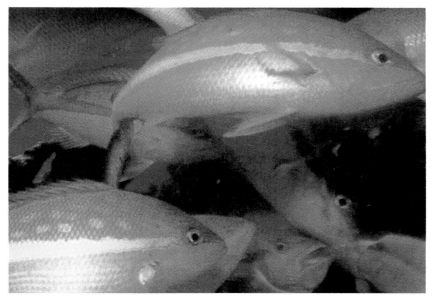

Ocyurus chrysurus. When fish school and act normally, they are usually healthy.

security. One or two plastic plants will serve a similar purpose, but keep things as simple as you can.

You should adjust the water conditions in the tank as close as possible to those in the main aquarium so that the risk of stress is minimal

only just prior to times when you contemplate adding more fishes to your community? I recommend that you keep the quarantine tank operational at all times. This gives you an immediate hospital facility for any of your main tank occupants should they become ill (assuming no fishes are being quarantined at that time).

Some aquarists use the water from the main tank to set up the quarantine tank, but this only has merit if you do not maintain the quarantine tank on a continuum. The problem with using water from an existing aquarium that includes fishes is that the water will almost certainly contain bacteria, some of which may be totally unfamiliar to the fishes being quarantined. The latter will of course have to encounter such bacteria once they are transferred, so it is a trade-off situation as to when this is least likely to adversely affect the fishes. Once you are very sure the fishes are well and eating properly, it would seem logical that this is the time to let them encounter the additional bacteria of the display tank rather than

when you are still not sure of their state of health.

Whether or not you routinely treat the fishes in the quarantine tank for the major diseases will clearly depend upon how well you trust the dealer where you purchased them. Reputable suppliers will make it very clear to you what the fishes have been treated for while in their care. However, certain diseases, such as velvet disease (caused by *Amblyoodinium*), can occur even after a dealer has screened for them. This is because they are both external and internal. The internal parasites are much more difficult to eradicate.

When all is said and done, quarantine periods are no guarantee that a fish is 100% healthy, because such a condition only holds good from one moment to the next. It can be changed by so many factors that are themselves changing

Microspathodon chrysurus, adult form. This fish has an anomaly on its back. It might be a well healed bite, but there is a chunk missing at the beginning of the dorsal (back) spines.

from one moment to the next. However, by practicing quarantine as a routine part of your husbandry, you weight the risks of keeping fishes healthy very much on your side of the equation, which is what it is all about.

FRESHWATER BATHS

The use of saltwater baths by freshwater aquarists is commonplace. Its merits in reverse are equally beneficial. Saltwater parasites absorb sea water to compensate for that lost from their cell(s) by osmosis. If they are placed into a freshwater situation they do not lose cell fluid but continue to absorb the fresh water until they literally burst. The fishes can tolerate such a water change for a longer period of time, and it is this fact that provides the merit of this cleansing process. However, even the marine fishes will die if left in fresh water for too long a time, because their cells are subject to the same effect.

If you have no quarantine tank, a freshwater bath will provide at least some means of ridding your fishes of parasites that are not buried under the mucous cells of the fish's skin. Even if a quarantine tank is available, a short freshwater bath will be useful in providing a quick cleansing of numerous pathogenic bacteria.

The bath is prepared by using tap water from which the chlorine has been removed. The pH and temperature must be the same as that of the display or quarantine tank. If they are not, the fish will be doubly shocked by the treatment and could die. The size of the bath need not be large–anything from a gallon up will be sufficient for one or two fishes. It is not essential that salt be added to the water, but many aquarists will add a little to make the bath just slightly saline.

When all is ready the fish is placed into the bath for a period of 2-5 minutes, or until the fish shows signs of distress. This length of time is all that is needed to eradicate *Amblyoodinium* and similar parasites (but longer periods are needed for other parasites) that are on the surface of the body and gills. Those embedded deeper in the dermis will need copper treatments (which can be obtained from your dealer). Bear in mind that fishes of differing species, age, health, and size will not react the same. Some will quickly turn onto their sides, others will panic and dart about. Some appear to adjust after a short while; others simply keel over and die if the exposure is too long for them. This is why you must watch the fishes as much as the clock and remove them when indicated.

Once the fishes have been so treated they can be placed into the quarantine tank or your main display tank, depending on the policy you are to adopt. A freshwater bath is also a sound idea for a fish being removed from an established tank because it needs to be treated for an illness. After the bath, it can then be given specialized treatment in the hospital tank. I am sure you will appreciate that the freshwater baths must take into account the condition of the fish. Clearly, if a fish is already in a bad way, a bath may not improve matters due to the shock effect. As with all treatments, you must apply a good measure of common sense in your approach to the situation you are confronted with. This means judging on an individual basis rather than on a general textbook method of procedure.

Thalassoma bifasciatum, male. The cloudy eye definitely indicates a problem. Usually it is polluted or poisoned water.

TREATMENTS

The modern treatments for ailing fishes are in the form of broad-spectrum antibiotics, as well as antiparasitic and antifungal drugs. Copper-based remedies, such as copper sulfate, copper acetate, and their likes, are very effective against many pathogens. Extreme caution is needed when using any of these preparations, because if the dosage is excessive it will kill the patient. Even at the correct dosage for the fish, it will almost certainly kill any invertebrates (a good reason to avoid invertebrates in the marine fish aquarium).

Microspathodon chrysurus. Normally, white spots indicate parasites, but these spots are characteristic of the juvenile form. See page 185 for the adult form.

Unless otherwise stated on the label, or directed by your vet, never use two drugs at the same time. This is because they may both contain a common compound which, together, will result in an overdose of that compound. Medicines may be placed into the aquarium, into foods, or may even be painted onto the skin of the fish in certain instances. In the last case, the size and nature of the fish will be an important pretreatment consideration, as such a treatment might unduly shock the fish.

The treatment of any marine fish is not without a degree of risk, but to do nothing is worse. Pay no attention to those who advocate "these matters often correct themselves." Such times as this may be true are remote indeed.

DIAGNOSIS

One of the major problems in attempting to treat a fish is in knowing what is wrong with it in the first place. Then comes the decision as to whether to treat the fish in the aquarium or to remove it to a hospital tank. Should the rest of the fishes in the tank also be treated,

even though they show no outward signs of the condition at that time? We can consider each of these aspects.

Diagnosis: The first thing that must be done is to check the water conditions. Often these are not good. The nitrite level may be too high, there may be a lack of oxygen, or the specific gravity may be incorrect. Under these conditions any fish is destined to be ill. Correction may bring about a rapid recovery. The clinical signs of an illness must be carefully noted. Based on all of the evidence, an attempt can then be made to diagnose the cause of the problem. The major signs of an illness will include the following, either in isolation or together. The more of them that are seen, the more serious the condition is.

1. The fish breathes abnormally (too fast or too slow).

2. The gills are swollen, are streaked with blood, or display minute dots on them. The color of the gills may have changed from their normal red.

3. The color of the fish is faded compared to its original color.

4. There are specks or spots on the fins and/or body.

5. The fins are ragged and/or blood streaked.

6. The eyes have a cloudy appearance or a whitish film over them.

7. The eyes are swollen or pop-eyed. The eyes are sunken.

8. There are lesions or ulcers on the body.

9. The scales are standing away from the body.

10. The belly is swollen.

11. The fish is swimming on its side.

12. The fish seems to have difficulty in holding its position in the water.

13. The fish is lying on the substrate.

14. The fish is gasping at the surface.

15. The fish is darting erratically about the tank or rubbing itself against coral, rocks, or other furnishings.

16. The fish is eating but is becoming emaciated.

17. The fish looks healthy but is not eating.

18. The fish has an obvious parasite(s) clinging to its body.

19. The fish has small or large swellings on its body.

20. There are cotton wool-like growths on some part(s) of the fish.

Having observed all of the outward signs of the illness, you should make a note of what the water conditions were when you first noticed that the fish was ill. Do not correct the water conditions without noting their original state (readings)–you must be very honest on these matters if you really wish to have a sound diagnosis. Other useful information to a vet or fish authority will be in regard to your feeding regimen, source of fish supply, when the last fish was added, when was the last illness in your aquarium, how rapid has the condition progressed, and have you already attempted to treat the fish with anything. Armed with all of this information, your local dealer or your vet should be able to counsel you with a course of action. It cannot be overstressed that to attempt a diagnosis without first making detailed notes is to court disaster. Many diseases display similar external signs. You normally cannot take the fish to the vet or the pet shop, so unless they make a house call (which is recommended) their advice will be based on the information you give them–a small

detail may thus be crucial in determining the treatment.

Where to Treat: There is no doubt that whenever possible any treatment for fishes is best done in a hospital tank. This overcomes many potential problems when adding medicines to the main aquarium water. It also removes the parasites from the rest of the tank community, thus at least limiting their effect. If it is decided to treat the main aquarium, this must be done under the supervision of an expert, otherwise all sorts of things could go wrong. If the illness proves a major one the aquarium will have to be stripped down and re-established, so the fishes will in any case have to be rehoused for a period of time.

Treat One or All: This decision will be determined by the nature of the problem and how soon it was identified. If only one fish appears to be affected, then it should be removed as quickly as possible so that it can be observed while a more detailed case history is prepared. The condition may not be one that will affect the other fishes. If a number of fishes seem to be suffering with the same symptoms, then it is best to assume that all the fishes have the illness and thus treat accordingly. If sufficient hospital tank facility is not available, either extra tanks must be prepared rapidly or you should accept the fact that the furnished display tank must be re-established. In this case you can remove as many of the furnishings as possible and use the display tank as the hospital tank. Ultimately, the fishes will still have to be transferred elsewhere while your aquarium is stripped, sterilized, and reestablished. All of this gives you good reason to be ever watchful of all matters where marine fishes are concerned.

Procedure: If only one or two fishes are ill they should be removed to the hospital tank immediately. At the same time, a partial water change (20-50%) of the main aquarium should be made, making sure that the temperature, pH, and SG of the added water are the same as that of the main aquarium (assuming this is correct). This will at least dilute any bacteria in the water. You may decide to give the fishes a freshwater bath before they are placed in the hospital tank. Once in the latter you can increase the temperature of the water by 1-4°C. This will tend to increase the rate at which the pathogens reproduce and will make the illness

Opposite: This fish is desperately ill from *Cryptocatyon* infestation. Copper sulfate can readily cure it. If untreated, the fish will perish.

more easily identified and treated.

Armed with your case history, you should then seek the advice of your supplier or vet. I would not advise the novice to attempt a diagnosis, much less treatment, until considerable experience has been gained in fishkeeping. Too many people do just this and the result is that their fishes live weeks or months rather than years.

MAJOR DISEASES AND CONDITIONS

The following diseases and conditions are those that are most frequently encountered in marine fish species. They are detailed so that the novice can become familiar with them and seek more detailed texts on their treatment and control than can be given in a general work such as this.

1. *Amblyoodinium ocellatum* (**Coral Fish or Velvet Disease**): This disease takes the form of tiny gray, white, or yellowish spots on the gills, body, and fins. It may also attack internal organs. If the spots can be seen the disease is already quite advanced. The fish will be breathing rapidly, as the gills are the prime locus of infection. Prior to the spots being visible, the fish will dart erratically about the tank and will try to rub itself against a rock. Treat with a proprietary medicine, following the label instructions carefully.

The protozoan flagellates that are the actual parasites are only one stage in the life cycle. They form cysts that are shed from the fish and multiply by simple cell division. These form new free-swimming flagellates that seek a new host. If they fail to find one within about 10 days they die. However, it has been established that some strains of *Amblyoodinium* have survived for four weeks without the presence of fishes or invertebrates. Never assume an unoccupied aquarium that previously contained either of these will be free of this parasite until at least six weeks have elapsed. Repeat treatment may be required in the event that internal flagellates cause a recurrence of the disease.

2. *Cryptocaryon irritans* (**Marine Ich**): This disease is in many ways similar to that produced by *Amblyoodinium.* However, the spots are larger when compared to those of the latter condition. Scratching is evident, but not as obvious. The disease spreads in the same manner, and should be treated in the same way as for velvet. Copper sulfate is a common remedy, but you should be aware that it will kill most invertebrates.

3. **Gill Parasites:** There are a number of these that may attack your fishes. They are usually trematodes or flukes. Usually, only large numbers will affect the fish, whose gills will become pink rather than red. The fish will breathe rapidly and the gills may be held open. Their greatest danger is the secondary infection that may result from the damage they cause. Treatment is usually with copper-based drugs.

A 15-minute freshwater or formaldehyde (1cc per gallon) bath may precede longer treatments in the hospital tank.

4. **Fin Rot:** This is a bacterial infection that results in the fins becoming ragged and eventually decomposing. In severe cases the rot will spread to the body, at which point there is little that can be done. In the early stages,

antibiotics may be successful, as may surgical trimming. The condition is often the result of poor water conditions, as well as being associated with other diseases. It provides a prime location for secondary infection.

5. **Cotton-wool Disease:** This is a fungal growth that appears on existing lesions. It manifests itself as a gray/white cotton-wool-like covering. Invariably poor water conditions are evident. If it is allowed to progress, the internal organs will be attacked and the fish will die. Correct the water conditions and treat for the underlying problem.

6. **Swim Bladder Problems:** There are many reasons why a fish may find it difficult to maintain its position in the water. The condition may simply be the result of poor diet, it may be due to chilling, it may be the result of a congenital disorder, or it may be associated with other diseases. Transfer the fish to a hospital tank and slowly raise the temperature. Reduce its food for a few days. If no improvement is seen seek expert advice.

7. **Treatment Poisoning:** In the event that an overdose of a treatment is given, the fish may float on the surface or lie on the substrate. The remedy relies on your quickly transferring it to a hospital tank. If it is already in the hospital tank, transfer it to another container of freshly made up salt water at the correct temperature, pH, and SG. It is wise to always have one of the proprietary water tonics that will immediately neutralize any copper in the water on hand; these are available from your dealer.

AFTER TREATMENT

Once a treatment has been successfully

This *Scatophagus* has developed a cotton-wool infection on a wound. it is easily treated with an antibiotic and a topical application of medicine (like iodine, malachite green, methylene blue, etc.).

administered it is important that the fish is fed and acclimatized to normalcy before it is returned to the display tank. If the temperature had been increased in a hospital tank, it must be reduced slowly so that the fish is not chilled or stressed. You must be very sure that the conditions in the main tank have been corrected if they were found unsuitable, otherwise you will be back at square one with repeat illnesses. After a major illness has affected a number of fishes, you would be wise to arrange for temporary accommodations for your fishes while you disinfect the aquarium.

Once a fish has been quarantined or treated in an isolation tank, the tank must of course be emptied and thoroughly cleaned before any other fishes are introduced. This applies even if quarantined fishes have proved to be very healthy. It is your attention to the seemingly chore-like jobs that will determine how successful you are at keeping marine fishes.

POSTMORTEM

Quite often, a fish may die without showing any external signs of an illness. In such instances it is beneficial to place the fish in a suitable container and contact your vet so that a postmortem can be carried out. If you have to retain the fish for a short while, it can be placed in the refrigerator–never the freezer. The cost of the postmortem will be amply repaid if it pinpoints a problem you can overcome, which may save others in your aquarium. It must be added that postmortems do not always reveal the cause of a problem, because pathogens often leave their host once it dies. The only evidence of their presence may be the damage to internal organs, but this does not always identify them specifically. Even so, the examination may enable your vet to make a professional guess at the problem.

Part of an aquarist's job of taking good care of his fishes is to know what they need and to know which ones don't normally make good candidates for the aquarium. Some of the most beautiful—and therefore highly desirable—species simply are not well suited to life in beginners' tanks and should be avoided by hobbyists with limited experience. *Zanclus cornutus,* the Moorish Idol, is one such species, as many newly captured individuals refuse to feed and waste away.

Marine Fish Species

In this chapter all of the fishes discussed are generally suitable for the community tank–some maybe more than others. It must be understood that while two species may live quite amicably in a given sized aquarium, they might be aggressive toward one another in a smaller tank. Comments in respect to compatibility are therefore of a general nature for the following reasons.

You may read that a species is a schooling fish, which may lead you to assume that the fish are friendly with each other. Two aspects arise out of this. First, the schooling formation may not be evident in your aquarium because the area of the wild school, or schooling formation, may be vastly greater than the size of your tank, so the fish do not appear to be in school formation. Secondly, because the space between each fish is restricted in the aquarium, the fish may squabble. In their wild habitat they are able to school while still keeping a given distance from each other.

Because it is virtually impossible to sex most marine species, and because so little is known about their breeding behavior, knowledge of these facts is important to aquarists, for these aspects of the fish's life influence their behavior in the aquarium. For example, at breeding time many animals change dramatically in their behavioral patterns. Normally peaceful animals can become very aggressive.

Coryphopterus lipernes

Coryphopterus personatus

Gobiosoma evelynae

Gobiosoma genie

Ioglossus helenae

Nes longus

Gobiodon histrio.

Cryptocentrus species.

It must be assumed that similar patterns exist in marine fishes, which might explain the sudden aggressive nature of a normally peaceful fish. In most colorful animals the color itself invariably has sexual as well as defensive implications. With this in mind, fish species of broadly similar colors and patterns are more likely to quarrel than those that have contrasting colors and markings (assuming the species are of a similar size). There is ample opportunity for even a novice to contribute information on the behavior patterns of marine fishes in captivity should careful notes be kept.

Most fishes are very territorial, the actual size of the territory they need being unknown to most marine aquarists. The territory may simply be an area within a few centimeters of a given rock or hiding place, or it may extend the length (or more) of your tank. If the tank is not large enough for a territory, and if two individuals of a species are placed in it, trouble is almost a certainty. One fish will bully the other, or they will constantly fight. In so doing they may disrupt the entire community of other fishes. It is for these reasons that you are always advised to understock your aquarium initially, even if it is biologically capable of housing more fishes. In this way the residents have the space to sort themselves out or not. You can then selectively add other fishes as you become more familiar with the behavior patterns of the resident fishes–you will become an experienced marine aquarist.

THE NAMES OF FISHES
Many living organisms are given two names.

One is their scientific name and the other is their common name. Every known organism has a scientific name, but some do not have common names because they may be extremely rare, so a common name has not, as yet, been applied to them. The scientific name of a fish is unique to it; no two species have the same name. However, this does not always hold true with common names, even within a given country. A fish can have any number of common names, but it can only have one scientific name.

While the latter point is true it should be added that a fish can be transferred from one genus to another. When this happens the first part of its scientific name will change. The scientific name is based on Latin or Greek and is composed of two parts. The first is the genus (pl. genera) and the second is the trivial or specific name. Only when the two are used together is a species identified. Once a species has been identified it may later be discovered that there are in fact a number of quite distinct forms of that species. The procedure is then as follows. The originally named species becomes the nominate race (or form) and its trivial name is repeated to form a trinomial. All other forms are given the same species name, but have their own trivial or trinomial added to this. For example, the species *Amphiprion frenatus* has a dark form which is regarded by some authorities as a species, *A. melanopus*. Others feel it is a subspecies of *A. frenatus*. If the latter is accepted then the original species becomes *A. frenatus frenatus*, while the dark form is the subspecies *A. frenatus melanopus*.

The classification of fishes in general, and marine fishes in

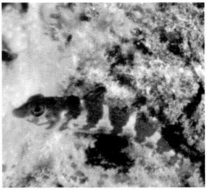

Redlip Blenny, *Ophioblennius atlanticus*

Saddled Blenny, *Malacoctenus triangulatus*

Bohlke's Blenny, *Malacoctenus boehlkei*

Bridled Goby, *Coryphopterus glaucofraenum*

Goldspot Blenny, *Gnatholepis thompsoni*

Colon Goby, *Coryphopterus dicrus*

particular, is constantly being revised in the light of new information, so it can appear to the beginner as a very complex subject. In reality it is basically very straightforward. It is the keeping up with the latest changes that creates the problems. You are advised to become familiar with the principles of classification (taxonomy) if you wish to became a serious aquarist.

In studying fishes you will need to be familiar with species names, as well as the families they are in.

The essence of the system is that the lowest rank in obligatory classification is that of a species. A number of similar species are placed in the same genus–they are a mutually collective group sharing many similar features. A number of similar genera are placed in a family, again based on the similarities they share. Families are brought together into orders, and orders into classes. The classes come together to form phyla (sing. phylum) and these, collectively, create the highest rank, that of the Kingdom Animalia. This includes all living animals, the plants comprising the other kingdom (assuming that bacteria, viruses, and their like are not given kingdom status, which some bacteriologists advocate should be the case).

Between the ranks mentioned there can be many subdivisions. Just how many are used, especially in the lower ranks, will depend on the zoologist and the situation. There are also "lumpers" and "splitters," as they are often referred to, who may group many taxa together or separate almost all of them, respectively. The species name is normally written in italics. The generic names always commence with a capital letter while the trivial name always commences with a lower case letter, as does the trinomial if this is applicable. After the species name, the person who first described the species (note: not necessarily the one who discovered it) may be cited. After this the date that the species was first described in a scientific journal may also be given. The journal itself may also be stated in a complete reference to the species. If a species has recently changed genera (or even its specific name), this is indicated by placing an equals (=) sign, together with the former name, in parentheses after the new name. Sometimes authors forget the = sign, which is unfortunate because this indicates that the name in parentheses is a subgenus rather than an alternative name. An example of the classification of the blue damselfish, *Chromis chromis*, follows.

Rank (Taxon)	Name	Features
KINGDOM	Animalia	All animals
PHYLUM	Chordata	Possess a dorsal central nerve chord
CLASS	Osteichthyes	Bony fishes
ORDER	Perciformes	Perch-like fishes
FAMILY	Pomacentridae	Single nostril, marine Forked caudal
GENUS	*Chromis*	Color differences
SPECIES	*Chromis chromis* (Linnaeus, 1758)	from others in the genus

(Note: The parentheses around Linnaeus indicate he was the original describer but placed the fish in a different genus.)

Chromis chromis

SPECIES DESCRIPTIONS

As the many color photographs throughout this book provide far better descriptions than can words, the information with respect to colors and markings is limited. The sizes quoted are average for the species in their native habitat. In the home aquarium the fishes will be rather smaller because fishes possess growth hormones that will limit their size when placed in restricted environments. They will of course still grow, and maybe even outgrow their aquarium, but they will never attain the size they would in their natural habitat.

The selection of species is necessarily restricted, given the confines of a single chapter. It does represent, however, a good sampling of the major families from which most beginners are likely to choose their initial stock. Some of the species included might not even be regarded as beginner fish by some aquarists. It is always a thorny decision as to which to include or which not to include when preparing texts. It often happens that a species regarded as being difficult and delicate by one marine keeper may not be found to be so by another. Much depends on the quality of the water and the diligence of the owner in preparing the overall ecosystem for the species chosen. A number of beginners prove to be natural fishkeepers, while many so-called experienced aquarists make the same mistakes year in and

Acanthurus japonicus

year out: their knowledge has not progressed in proportion to the years they may have kept fishes.

A number of species that can be kept in either single species or community tanks have been deliberately excluded. Some are just too large, some secrete poisons into the water if suddenly frightened, and some possess very dangerous spines, so are best left until additional experience has been gained. Even among those fishes included, for example triggerfishes, the beginner should exercise extreme care when handling the fishes in order to avoid painful jabs. Always try to catch fishes by using containers and driving the fish into them with small nets.

The fish species are arranged in alphabetical order by families. This enables you to locate the latter more quickly when wanting to check on a particular group of fishes.

The accompanying table indicates the orders and suborders of the various families. Finally, a second table lists the species alphabetically (by genus) and indicates their family so you can easily cross reference them.

In some instances no species are described, the family description being a guide to their general type, feeding, and dispositions.

1. ACANTHURIDAE - SURGEONFISHES AND TANGS

These broadly discshaped fishes require a good supply of algae which they will browse on for long periods. Some are peaceful but many are rather aggressive, especially toward their own kind. Most are armed with a spine(s) on the side of their caudal

Orders, Suborders, and Families of Fishes
Cited in the Text

ORDER	SUBORDER	FAMILY
Perciformes	Acanthuroidei	Acanthuridae
	Blennioidei	Blenniidae
	Gobioidei	Gobiidae
	Labroidei	Labridae
	Percoidei	Apogonidae
		Chaetodontidae
		Pornacanthidae
		Monodactylidae
		Pomacentridae
		Serranidae
Tetraodontiformes	Balistoidei	Balistidae
		Monacanthidae
Gasterosteiformes	Syngnathoidei	Syngnathidae

Alphabetical List of Species in Text,
with their Family & Group Names
(Families in alphabetical order in text)

SPECIES	FAMILY	GROUP NAME
Acanthurus coeruleus *japonicus* *leucosternon* *lineatus* *nigricans*	Acanthuridae	Surgeonfishe & Tangs
Amphiprion bicinctus *ephippium* *frenatus* *ocellaris* *polymnus*	Pomacentridae	Clownfishes
Anthias squamipinnis	Serranidae	Basses & Groupers

Apogon maculatus	Apogonidae	Cardinalfishes
Aspidontus taeniatus	Blenniidae	Blennies
Balistapus undulatus	Balistidae	Triggerfishes
Centropyge bicolor	Pomacanthidae	Angelfishes
flavissimus		
heraldi		
loriculus		
Chaetodon auriga	Chaetodontidae	Butterflyfishes
semilarvatus		
vagabundus		
Chromis viridis	Pomacentridae	Damselfishes
xanthturus		
Chrysiptera cyanea	Pomacentridae	Damselfishes
Coris gaimard	Labridae	Wrasses, Rainbowfishes
Dascyllus aruanus	Pomacentridae	Damselfishes, Humbugs
trimaculatlus		
Gobiosoma oceanops	Gobiidae	Gobies
Gramma loreto	Serranidae	Basses & Groupers
Heniochus acuminatus	Chaetodontidae	Butterflyfishes
Hippocampus kuda	Syngnathidae	Seahorses, Pipefishes
Labroides dimidiatus	Labridae	Wrasses, Rainbowfishes
Monodactylus argenteus	Monodactylidae	Fingerfishes
Oxymonacanthus	Monacanthidae	Filefishes
longirostris		
Paracanthurus hepatus	Acanthuridae	Surgeonfishes & Tangs
Pomacanthus imperator	Pomacanthidae	Angelfishes
paru		
Pseudochromis	Serranidae	Basses & Groupers
paccagnellae		
Sphaeramia nematoptera	Apogonidae	Cardinalfishes
Stegastes leucostictus	Pomacentridae	Damselfishes
Zebrasoma flavescens	Acanthuridae	Surgeonfishes & Tangs
veliferum		
xanthurum		

Acanthurus coeruleus

peduncle (the area just before the tail). These can inflict serious wounds on other fishes. Although they are schooling fishes, you would need a large aquarium to house a number of individuals. If kept, they should either be as individual specimens or as groups of five or more. Two or three in a tank will invariably start quarreling with each other over territorial rights. They may also not take kindly to new additions to an aquarium. Although basically herbivorous, they can forage on the substrate for food. A number of them display beautiful coloration– unfortunately, these are usually the hardest to care for.

la. ***Acanthurus coeruleus***
Blue Tang.
Distribution: Tropical western Atlantic.
Size: 30cm (12in), about half this in the aquarium.

Description: The juvenile form is yellow with blue edges to the dorsal and anal fins; blue eye ring present. Adults are blue with darker longitudinal stripes.

Comment: juveniles are rather quarrelsome; adults are more sociable.

1b. *Acanthurus japonicus*

Goldrim, Lipstick, or White-cheeked Tang or Surgeonfish.

Distribution: Tropical western Pacific.

Size: 18cm (7in).

Description: Olive yellow, white cheek patches, vertical yellow bar in caudal fin. Some orange in rear of dorsal fin.

Comment: Peaceful. Very similar in color to *A. nigricans*.

1c. *Acanthurus leucosternon*

Powder Blue or Whitebreasted Tang or Surgeonfish.

Distribution: Tropical Indo-Pacific.

Acanthurus leucosternon.

Size: 30cm (11.5in). Barely more than 50% of this in captivity.

Description: Variable light blue body color. Black mask, white breast, dorsal fin yellow, the color extending into peduncle.

Comment: Best kept as a single specimen in a community tank.

1d. *Acanthurus lineatus*

Blue-lined, Pajama or Clown Tang or Surgeonfish.

Distribution: Tropical Indo-Pacific.

Size: 20cm (8in), rarely more than 15cm (6in) in the home aquarium.

Description: Ground color yellow. Longitudinal blue stripes edged with black. Ventral area white.

Comment: Best kept as single specimen in community tank or as a group in a species tank, where quarrelsome nature may not be as evident. A very striking fish.

1e. *Paracanthurus hepatus*

Regal, Blue, Flagtail, or Wedge-tailed Blue Tang or Surgeonfish.

Distribution: Tropical Indo-Pacific.

Size: 26cm (10in), about half this in the home aquarium.

Description: A very striking fish with blue ground color and black edges to fins, as well as a black palette shape on body. Wedge of caudal fin is vivid yellow.

Comment: Hardier than its bright colors might suggest.

1f. *Zebrasoma flavescens*

Yellow Tang or Surgeonfish.

Distribution: Tropical Indo-Pacific.

Size: 20cm (8in), but will be about 30%, smaller in the aquarium.

Description: Yellow! It sports white scalpels on the peduncle. Large dorsal and anal fins. Well developed snout.

Comment: Keep as

Above: *Acanthurus lineatus.* **Below:** *Zebrasoma xanthurum.*

Above: *Acanthurus nigricans.* **Below**: *Paracanthurus hepatus* and the Yellowtail Blue Tang, *Acanthurus coeruleus.*

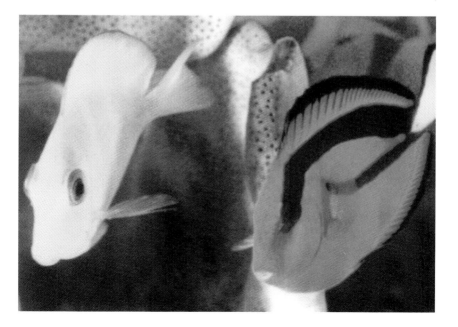

single species or a group of five or more to reduce risk of quarreling. Good algae grazers.

1g. *Zebrasoma veliferum*

Striped Sailfin Tang or Surgeonfish.

Distribution: Tropical Indo-Pacific.

Size: 35cm (14in), about half this in the aquarium.

Description: A very variable species in terms of its colors and pattern. Adults are shades of brown in vertical stripes. Mask spotted with cream-brown. Dorsal and anal fins very large and also striated. Juveniles lack spotting; the vertical bands are much broader and may be black or brown on a brown-green ground.

Comment: Best obtained as juveniles when they will adjust better to aquarium life (this applies to all tangs).

1h. *Zebrasoma xanthurum*

Yellow-tailed, Emperor, or Purple Sailfin Tang or Surgeonfish.

Distribution: Red Sea to Arabian Gulf.

Size: 20cm (8in).

Description: Indigo blue to brown through yellow brown with yellow caudal fin. Red-brown mask spots.

Comment: Attractive species if the coloration is good. Similar to most other tangs in terms of its nature.

2. APOGONIDAE–CARDINALFISHES

The cardinalfishes are not quite as colorful as many other marine species, this reflecting their nocturnal habits. They possess large eyes and, unusually for marine fishes, two dorsal fins. They are shy and should not be included with very active fishes, especially in the smaller aquarium. They like a well furnished tank that provides darkened places of refuge. Do not expose them to bright light initially, but increase the intensity during their quarantine period. They are omnivorous but are not especially fond of flake foods. Feed in the evening.

2a. ***Apogon maculatus***
Flamefish.
Distribution: Tropical West Atlantic.
Size: 15cm (6in), up to 10cm in aquariums.
Description: Red body. Two white horizontal lines through eyes. Black spot below second dorsal fin, another behind eyes.
Comment: Peaceful inhabitants of a community tank. Do not include them with boisterous, large fishes. Provide plenty of hiding places in low levels of the aquarium.

2b. ***Sphaeramia nematoptera***
Pennant, Pajama, Banded, or Spotted Cardinalfish.
Distribution: Tropical Indo-Pacific.
Size: 10cm (4in), smaller in an aquarium.
Description: Variable yellowish ground color with red-brown spots on body behind the first dorsal. Dark band spotted with dull yellow from first dorsal to pelvic fins. Eyes red.

3. **BALISTIDAE– TRIGGERFISHES**
With their set-back eyes and protruding jaws, the triggerfishes always fascinate onlookers. They are rather large fishes for a novice to take on, but most are purchased as juvenile specimens. Some may be peaceful, but many are very aggressive, especially to their own kind. They have sharp teeth and devour starfishes and other invertebrates that are unfortunate enough to be in the same locality. They will as

Above: *Zebrasoma flavescens.* **Below:** *Zebrasoma veliferum.*

Above: *Apogon maculatus.* **Below:** *Sphaeramia nematoptera.*

readily devour other fishes! Their diet is basically carnivorous, but some will take green food items. They are very intelligent and can become very tame, which accounts for their popularity. Best kept as individual tank occupants until experience is gained and a large aquarium is available. Their common name is derived from the fact that their first dorsal fin spine can be raised and locked into position. This makes them an uncomfortable meal for large predatory fishes, which may quickly spit them out once in their mouths! The erect spine is also used to wedge themselves into crevices, making them difficult for the aquarist to catch. Nonetheless, caves and crevices should be available to them. They are relatively slow swimmers.

3a. ***Balistapus undulatus***

Undulated or Red or Orange-lined Triggerfish.

Distribution: Tropical Indo-Pacific.

Size: 30cm (12in), a little over half this in captivity.

Description: Green ground color with yellow striations. These may be orange-red on the lower parts of the body. Caudal fin yellow.

Comment: Very aggressive toward its own kind and other fishes of its size or smaller. Becomes tame quickly, a fact that has made it popular with many aquarists. Keep singly as a pet unless a very large aquarium is available to include it with larger species. The same remarks hold true for *Sufflamen bursa*, *Balistes vetula*, and others which are often offered for sale at reasonable prices. *Melichthys ringens*, the

Black or Black-finned Triggerfish, is possibly one of the more tolerant of this group of fishes. But it is also rather drab in its coloration, being mainly brown with black fins and some white edging to body and caudal fin.

4. **BLENNIIDAE– BLENNIES**

The blennies are elongate fishes with very long dorsal fins. They require plenty of hiding places, as many are rather shy creatures. This said, some are also very aggressive and may even take bites out of larger fishes. Select the species with care. Omnivorous diet. Coloration is usually rather drab compared to most marine species. There are over 50 genera but only about 5 are of interest to the tropical marine enthusiast. One to watch out for is *Aspidontus taeniatus*,

the False Cleanerfish or Sabertooth Blenny. It is very predatory and will approach larger fishes that do not suspect it is about to take a piece out of them. They think it is the cleaner wrasse *Labroides dimidiatus*.

5. **CHAETODONT– IDAE—BUTTERFLYFISHES**

This family, as far as practical management goes, is much the same as family Pomacanthidae, the angelfishes. They are very beautiful fishes. Possibly more so than pomacanthids, the chaetodontids can be very difficult to acclimatize to the aquarium and to get them to feed. Some are tolerant and relatively peaceful fishes, others are aggressive, especially with their own kind. Once established in an aquarium they can thrive, but soon deteriorate if the water quality drops. They cannot be regarded as

Above: *Balistapus undulatus.* **Below:** *Sufflamen bursa.*

Above: *Melichthys niger.* **Below:** *Aspidontus taeniatus.*

easy fishes for a beginner to start with, but some species will be seen In your local dealer's tanks. Be sure you see them feeding if you are tempted to purchase one.

5a. *Chaetodon auriga*

Threadfin Butterflyfish.

Distribution: Tropical Indo-Pacific and Red Sea.

Size: 20cm (8in), a little over half this in the aquarium.

Description: White ground merging to yellow posteriorly. Black vertical stripe on head forming mask. Dark lines meeting at right angles on body. Black spot on dorsal fin. Snout developed.

Comment: Relatively peaceful. Needs plenty of hiding places. One of the more hardy butterflyfishes.

5b. *Chaetodon semilarvatus*

Yellow Butterflyfish.
Distribution: Red Sea.

Size: 20cm (8i-n), a little over half this in the aquarium.

Description: Ground color yellow. Vertical narrow bands of brown orange. Blue-black patch on cheeks that extends around rear part of eye. Narrow blue stripes inside edges of dorsal and anal fins.

Comments: Very striking fish that will accept its own kind in large aquarium. Rather delicate so not an ideal beginner's choice.

5c. *Chaetodon vagabundus*

Vagabond or Crisscross Butterflyfish.

Distribution: Tropical Indo-Pacific.

Size: 20cm (8in).

Description: Cream ground color with brown striations meeting at right angles. Black band runs through the eye. Black band from dorsal fin, across caudal peduncle, and ending in anal fin. Yellow in caudal fin and soft dorsal and anal fins.

Comment: Possibly the hardiest of the butterflyfishes, which makes up for its lack of vivid coloration. Suited to the novice and the community aquarium.

5d. *Heniochus acuminatus*

Wimplefish, Bannerfish, Royal Coachman, Poor Man's Moorish Idol, or Pennant Coralfish.

Distribution: Indo-Pacific and Red Sea.

Size: 20cm (8in), smaller in an aquarium.

Description: Superficially resembles *Zanclus cornutus*, the Moorish Idol. Ground color silvery white with two wide vertical black bands through body region. Fins large, dorsal ending in a long filament.

Comment: Peaceful and easy to maintain. Can be kept in small groups of 3-5. Water must, however, be very clean.

6. GOBIIDAE– GOBIES

This is a large family of fishes whose members mostly inhabit the shallow warmer waters. They also frequent rock pools, and certain ones can survive out of water for periods of time as they scramble from one pool to another. Some species live in fresh water. They are elongate fishes that require lots of hiding places near the substrate. A number of species are surprisingly colorful, and many are interesting and peaceful little fishes. Their diet is essentially carnivorous (invertebrates), but they will happily take commercial foods as well as bits of meat. They will live happily alongside their own kind and other fishes, making them delightful

Left: *Chaetodon auriga.* **Below:** *Chaetodon semilarvatus.*

Right: *Heniochus acuminatus.*
Below: *Chaetodon vagabundus.*

members of either community or specialized tanks. Their drawback is that at this time they are not very long lived. They also require somewhat cooler waters than most other marine species you are likely to keep.

6a. *Gobiosoma oceanops*

Neon Goby.

Distribution: Tropical western Atlantic.

Size: 6cm (2.5in), smaller in aquariums.

Description: Elongate cylindrical body. Black on dorsal surface with deep neon blue longitudinal band on either side of body, extending onto snout.

Comment: A justifiably popular aquarium inhabitant. This species provides a cleaner service to larger fishes, removing parasites from their body. It is a good community member, but shy if lively and food-competitive fishes are also resident. One of the marine species that are bred in aquariums. They prefer a slightly cooler water temperature than fishes of the Indo-Pacific, but are adaptable if this is done slowly in the quarantine tank.

There are many other gobies that may be seen on the lists of dealers, depending on where you live. They range from yellow to vivid reds with blue bands, and from almost black to mottled browns. Be sure to check on the preferred water temperatures of species offered, and be sure to provide ample hiding places.

7. LABRIDAE– WRASSES OR RAINBOWFISHES

This family boasts about 500 members. The typical shape is elongate. Many of the species exhibit quite beautiful colors and markings, made the more interesting because those of the juvenile and adult can be totally different. Even different sexes of the same species can sport differing colors. The negative side of the wrasses is that most of them are very large fishes and may outgrow your aquarium if they live long enough. Their diet is carnivorous-small crustaceans and live foods, though some vegetable matter is taken. Most are peaceful fishes but will eat any very small fishes. Some are cleaner species, taking parasites from larger fishes.

7a. ***Coris gaimard***

Clown Wrasse, Gaimard's Rainbowfish, Tomato Wrasse, or Red Labrid.

Distribution: Tropical Indo-Pacific.

Size: 30cm (12in), about half this size in aquariums.

Description: This depends on the age of the fish, as colors and patterns, as in many other labrids, change with maturity. The juvenile is orange with a few dark edged white blotches and bars on the upper body. The body colors slowly darken and the white disappears with maturity. The adult is brownish and covered with small violet spots and greenish streaks on the facial area. You would never know these young and adults were the same species, a comment true in many other marine species.

Comments: Best kept as single specimens in the community tank as all *Coris* species are loners by nature. They need a soft substrate to dig into at night. Very active during the daytime.

7b. ***Labroides dimidiatus***

Cleaner Wrasse, Brindle Beauty, Blue-streak Wrasse.

Above: *Gobiosoma oceanops.* **Below:** *Labroides dimidiatus.*

Coris gaimard. The juvenile, in the photo above, barely resembles the adult coloration shown in the photo below.

Distribution: Tropical Indo-Pacific and Red Sea.

Size: 10cm (4in), smaller in aquariums.

Description: Elongate body is a light blue. Black or dark blue horizontal band from tail to snout, wider at the posterior end. Juveniles are black with a neon blue band. The mouth is terminal and is the means of distinguishing it from the predatory false cleanerfish, *Aspidontus taeniatus* (see Family 4). The latter has an underslung mouth.

Comment: A very useful fish to have in the community aquarium because it will rid larger fishes of external parasites, thus its common name. The fishes stay motionless in order to allow the cleaner to pick the parasites from their body and even from within their mouths. It is an easy fish to care for, taking most foods readily. Overnight the cleanerfish seeks out a coral or similar hiding place and secretes a mucous cocoon in which to sleep.

8. MONACANTHIDAE FILEFISHES

This group of species is now regarded by most authorities as being members of the family Balistidae, the triggerfishes. Refer to that family for general information. The filefishes are rather smaller than triggerfishes and considerably less aggressive. Indeed, they are rather timid and less tolerant of changing water conditions. Their diet is more herbivorous, but still omnivorous. Once settled in a community they are quite peaceful. They could also be kept in a single species tank in small numbers.

8a. *Oxymonacanthus longirostris*

Long-nosed, Orangegreen, or Orange

Emerald Filefish; Beaked Leatherjacket.

Distribution: Tropical Indo-Pacific.

Size: 10cm. (4in).

Description: Ground color is blue-green on which are rows of large orange spots. The "file" (first dorsal fin spine) is yellow. Eyes have six bluish spoke-like pattern bars. Snout well developed.

Comment: A sociable species that can be kept in pairs or small numbers. Rather delicate and will not appreciate very active fishes in their presence.

9. **MONODACTYL-IDAE—FINGERFISHES**

Although quite large when fully grown, fingerfish imported for the aquarium will be smaller. They are very hardy species and can withstand both brackish and fresh water. They are able to survive in waters that would kill most marines. Omnivorous,

they are excellent scavengers, taking just about any food offered to them, making them an easy fish to care for. Not especially colorful, they are nonetheless worthwhile inhabitants of a community tank. Their drawback is that they are extremely active fish, which may not be to the liking of more timid and slow-moving residents.

9a. ***Monodactylus argenteus***

Silver Dollar, Singapore or Malayan Angel, or Fingerfishes.

Distribution: Tropical Indo-Pacific and Red Sea.

Size: 23cm (9in), usually only half this in the aquarium.

Description: Body silvery with two vertical black bands forward of the dorsal fin. Fins yellow. Bilaterally compressed disc shape.

Comment: Very easy to care for schooling species. Very active, so they prefer a large

Above: *Oxymonacanthus longirostris.* **Below:** *Monodactylus argenteus.*

Right: *Centropyge bicolor.* **Below:** *Centropyge heraldi.*

aquarium. Young specimens can be kept in fresh or brackish waters, but best suited to salt water once mature.

10.

POMACANTHIDAE– ANGELFISHES

This group of fishes can be summed up in two words, gorgeous and difficult. A number of species grow very large indeed. Most are territorial and may exhibit bullying tendencies toward other fishes, as well as their own kind. Some are almost herbivorous in their diet, but most are omnivorous. They delight in feasting on any invertebrates you may place in the aquarium, though they are not as bad as their close relatives, the butterflyfishes, in this respect. They require places of refuge to retreat to overnight. Angelfishes are very intolerant to changes in water conditions. If you decide to have one or two, be very sure you maintain the water quality or you will find their acquisition a costly experience! There are a number of small angels, and these are the best to start with. In a large aquarium with excellent water conditions, angels can become very tame and live for many years, so you can see their colors change as they mature.

10a. ***Centropyge bicolor***

Blue-yellow, or Bicolored Angel, or Bicolored Cherub.

Distribution: Tropical Indo-Pacific.

Size: 7.5cm (3in).

Description: Front half of body, also caudal fin, yellow. Remainder of fish is a dark blue and there is a blue bar across the head region between the eyes.

Comment: A magnificent fish, but it is rather delicate until established. Retains similar color from young to maturity. Can be kept in small groups because the miniature angels are not as aggressive as their larger relatives. A similar sized fish is the Pygmy or Caribbean Dwarf Angelfish. This is totally dark blue, but with a fiery orange to the fore-snout and breast.

10b. **Centropyge loriculus**

Flame Angelfish.

Distribution: Tropical Pacific Ocean.

Size: 10cm (4in), somewhat smaller in an aquarium.

Description: Deep orange face, dorsal, and ventral areas. Mid-body is golden with vertical black bars. Posterior ends of dorsal and anal fins black barred with blue or violet. A most impressive fish.

Comment: Another sociable miniature that takes an omnivorous diet and would be a jewel in the smaller aquarium. If you prefer a yellow angelfish there are two that will delight you. *Centropyge heraldi*, Herald's Angelfish, and *C. flavissimus*, the Lemonpeel Angelfish, both grow to about 10cm (4in) in the wild. These are more herbivorous than the previous species and make fine community tank species.

10c. **Pomacanthus imperator**

Emperor or Imperial Angelfish.

Distribution: Tropical Indo-Pacific.

Size: 40cm (16in), maybe to 75%, of this in the aquarium.

Description: juveniles (up to about 10cm) have a dark blue ground color on which are black and white complete and incomplete rings. The adults have a lighter blue ground on which there are 20-30

Above: *Centropyge loriculus.* **Below:** *Pomacanthus paru.*

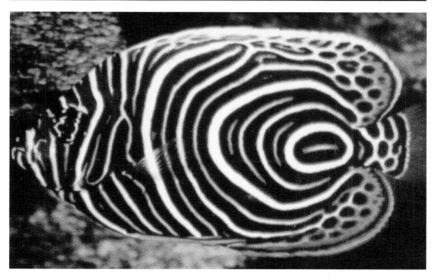

Many coral fishes completely change color between their juvenile form and their adult dress. This is especially true of *Pomacanthus imperator*. The immature coloration is shown above; the adult form is illustrated below.

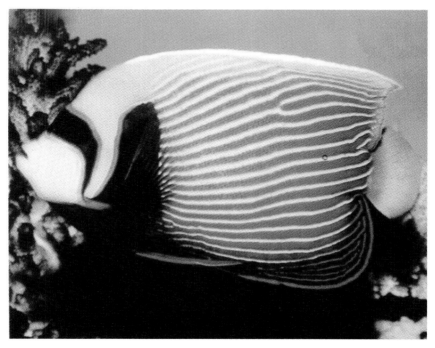

longitudinal yellow bands, one or more of which may be forked. The caudal fin is yellow and the anal fin dark blue with blue lines.

Comment: A regal fish indeed. If you plan to rear this species from immature to adult you must have a very large aquarium.

10d. ***Pomacanthus paru***

French Angelfish.

Distribution: Tropical western Atlantic.

Size: 30cm (12in).

Description: Juvenile black-brown with four vertical yellow bands. These become white and eventually disappear. The black becomes brown ticked with beige. The adult is brown-gray with beige to white ticks and a gray mouth.

Comment: As a juvenile, this species performs a cleaner service to other fishes. This is not always appreciated in the aquarium if the species are not compatible in terms of their distribution area. In this instance the other species may feel the angel is aggressive. It is a hardy and long-lived species under the right conditions.

11. **POMACENTRIDAE– CLOWNFISHES AND DAMSELFISHES**

The fishes of this family are probably the most popular marine fishes kept in aquariums. They are of small size, highly colorful, and very hardy—especially the damselfishes. Many make fine community fishes, though some may be rather belligerent toward their own kind in settling territorial rights. As marine fishes go, the very popular species are modest in price. The clownfishes are also known as anemonefishes due to their close association with these invertebrates. There are numerous species to choose from and they are all omnivorous in their diet. The damselfishes of the genus *Dascyllus* are among the fishes in which audible sounds, in the form of clicks, can be heard when they communicate in defending their territories.

11a. *Amphiprion bicinctus*

Two Banded, or Banded Clownfish, or Red Sea Anemonefish.

Distribution: Red Sea.

Size: 12cm (4.5in), about 7.6cm (3in) in aquariums.

Description: Dark brown to golden brown body with three vertical white bands in the juvenile, but only two in the adult (that on the peduncle disappears). Fins yellow-orange, snout and breast orange.

Comment: Less aggressive toward its own kind than some other anemonefishes. As with other anemonefishes, it is not essential that anemones are present in the aquarium for the fish to prosper–though naturally their presence will make the fish feel more secure.

11b. *Amphiprion ephippium*

Tomato, Fire, or Red Saddleback Clownfish.

Distribution: Tropical Indo-Pacific.

Size: 12cm (4.5in), smaller in aquariums.

Description: Juveniles are red with a black edged white vertical band behind the head. This is lost in the adult.

Comment: May be rather belligerent toward its own kind. There are other similar clownfishes, including *A. frenatus*, that retain the white head band as an adult.

11c. *Amphiprion ocellaris*

Common or Percula

Amphiprion ephippium is shown above. *Amphiprion bicinctus* is shown below.

Above: *Amphiprion frenatus*. **Below:** *Amphiprion polymnus.*

Clownfish.

Distribution: Tropical Indo-Pacific.

Size: 9cm (3.5in), about 5cm (2in) in the aquarium.

Description: Orange with three black-edged, broad white bands encircling the body.

Comment: This is the most commonly sold clownfish. It may be very aggressive toward its own kind, but much depends on the size of the aquarium. A darker colored threebanded clownfish is the Maroon Clownfish, *Premnas biaculeatus*. It has a large spine below each eye.

11d. *Amphiprion polymnus*

White-saddled or Saddleback Clownfish.

Distribution: Tropical western Pacific.

Size: 12cm (4.5in), slightly smaller in the aquarium.

Description: Dark red-brown to black body, lighter snout and breast, extending into pelvics. White band behind eyes over head and white saddle on back and sides. White edging to caudal and dorsal fins.

Comment: Not so commonly available, and rather more difficult to establish, this is a species for the more expert clownfish enthusiasts.

11e. *Chrysiptera cyanea*

Blue Devil Damselfish.

Distribution: Tropical western Pacific.

Size: 6cm (2.4in).

Description: Royal blue with darker blue edging in the fins and on the snout.

Comment: There are many blue damselfishes. Labels on dealers' tanks are not always correct–which is not helped any by the fact that ichthyologists often disagree on the status and generic name of a given species. However, they are all fascinating and desirable little fishes whose only drawback is that some will squabble among themselves more than others. This species is reasonably tolerant, especially in groups. *Pomacentrus caeruleus*, the Yellowbellied Blue Devil, is somewhat larger and more argumentative when mature.

11f. *Chromis xanthurus*

Pale-tailed Chromis.

Distribution: Tropical Indo-west Pacific.

Size: 15cm (6in), half this size in the aquarium.

Description: Brown with white caudal fin, the white extending variably past the peduncle.

Comment: Like other members of its genus, this species is sociable with its conspecifics; indeed, it is best in small groups. This is not so of all related species. *Pomacentrus philippinus*, for example, is quite pugnacious, and this may extend to any similarly colored fishes. This does add a slight complication when obtaining stock from differing sources, and which are labeled as the same species.

Chromis species all have deeply forked caudal fins which might help in identification. The common Atlantic damselfish is the Beau Gregory, *Stegastes leucostictus*. This is blue on the dorsal surface and yellow on the ventral. It is territorial but hardy.

11g. *Chromis viridis*

Blue-green Chromis.

Distribution: Tropical Indo-west Pacific.

Size: 10cm (4in), about this size in the aquarium.

Description: Variable amounts of green on body. The color extends into the caudal fin, less so on other finnage.

Comments: Keep these fish in small

Above: *Amphiprion ocellaris.* **Below:** *Chrysiptera cyanea.*

Above: *Chromis xanthura.* **Below:** *Chromis viridis.*

groups, they will feel happier. Single specimens tend to become nervous and thus rather shy.

11h. *Dascyllus aruanus*

Three Banded, Striped or White-tailed Humbug.

Distribution: Tropical Indo-Pacific.

Size: 8cm (3in).

Description: Disc shaped. White ground with three wide vertical bands which extend into fins. The rear two bands are joined by a bar of black running along the edge of the dorsal fin. Tail transparent.

Comment: A very hardy species. They live in pairs or in groups. The latter, however, once established, will not readily accept newcomers of their species-which they will promptly attack. Very similar is *D. melanurus*, the Four Band or Black-tailed Humbug. The bands are more vertical in this species. The second and third bars are not connected in the dorsal fin, while the fourth band is in the caudal fin.

11i. *Dascyllus trimaculatus*

Domino or Three-spot Humbug; Three or Whitespot Puller.

Distribution: Tropical Indo-Pacific.

Size: 15cm (6in), up to half this in the aquarium.

Description: Velvety black when young, becoming grayer with age. White spot on forehead and one on each flank in upper mid-body, just below dorsal fin. The head spot may disappear in later life.

Comment: Associates with anemones when young. This is a hardy species whose drawback lies in the fact it gets rather aggressive as it matures.

12. SERRANIDAE– SEA BASSES AND GROUPERS

One member of this

family is over six feet long and can top 700lb in weight. However, most are much smaller–but all are predatory. Many have quite exquisite coloration and patterns, ensuring that they will always attract the marine aquarist. Select with care for the community tank. Be aware that even some of the small species may take a cheeky nip at the fins of larger fishes. Even though they are not a threat to them, this can unsettle slow moving peaceful fishes. The diet is basically meat in any form.

12a. ***Anthias squamipinnis***

Lyretail Coralfish, Wreckfish, Orange Sea Perch.

Distribution: Tropical Indo-Pacific and Red Sea.

Size: 12.5cm (5in), rarely this large in the aquarium.

Description: Basic color a warm pinkish red. Areas of gold on flanks with some silver. Some extended rays in front part of dorsal fin, especially in the male.

Comment: A peaceful schooling species best kept in groups in a large aquarium.

12b. ***Gramma loreto***
Royal Gramma.

Distribution: Caribbean Sea.

Size: 10cm (4in), about 7.5cm (3in) in the aquarium.

Description: Front two thirds of body are violet magenta, the rear third is a golden yellow. There is a black spot in the front part of the dorsal fin, and a black bar extends from mouth through the eye.

Comment: A truly magnificent fish, but one that should not be included with unduly active species. It is a cave-dwelling species that will not tolerate others near its chosen home among the rocks, especially its own kind. Easy to care for and

Dascyllus aruanus, above. **Below:** *Dascyllus trimaculatus.*

Anthias squamipinnis, above. **Below:** *Gramma loreto.*

feed, as its diet is very cosmopolitan. Very similar in color, but lacking the black marks, and with no color extending into the fins, is the False Gramma or Paccagnella's Dottyback, *Pseudochromis paccagnellae*. There are numerous other small and colorful members of this family, but they are all rather delicate.

13. SYNGNATHIDAE– SEAHORSES AND PIPEFISHES

If there is one marine fish most people can recognize it is the seahorse (though the average person does not always appreciate that it is actually a fish). Pipefishes are elongate with a similar long snout and a less armored-looking body. Both seahorses and pipefishes are peaceful fishes, but both are carnivorous. They require a diet of small live foods, such as *Daphnia*, fish fry, and brine shrimp. The seahorse requires a means of attachment for its prehensile tail; sea fans or corals are normally used. Although the seahorse is well suited to a community tank with quite peaceful fishes, it is also ideal for the single-species tank. Certain pipefishes are quite hardy and can survive in a variety of salinity concentrations almost down to fresh water.

13a. *Hippocampus kuda*

Yellow, Oceanic, or Spotted Seahorse.

Distribution: Tropical Indo-Pacific.

Size: 30cm (12in) (vertical dimension), much smaller in the aquarium.

Description: Variable. They may be gray-black when first introduced but slowly become yellow as they settle down. If they later become gray this usually indicates something is amiss.

Comment: Best kept

in single-species tank where there is no competition for food from more active fishes. Many species readily breed in aquariums. An unusual aspect of their breeding is that the male carries the developing embryos. The eggs are inserted into his pouch by the female during mating. There are numerous species of seahorses offered for sale from various parts of the world. They range in color from brown-black through olive-brown to red and yellow. Longevity is usually from 1-4 years.

Pipefishes are found in many seas, oceans, and even some brackish waters from the Baltic Sea to the Indian Ocean. Their needs are the same as for seahorses. They are better swimmers than the latter, and if placed in a community aquarium it must be with slow-moving fishes that will not make them nervous.

Index